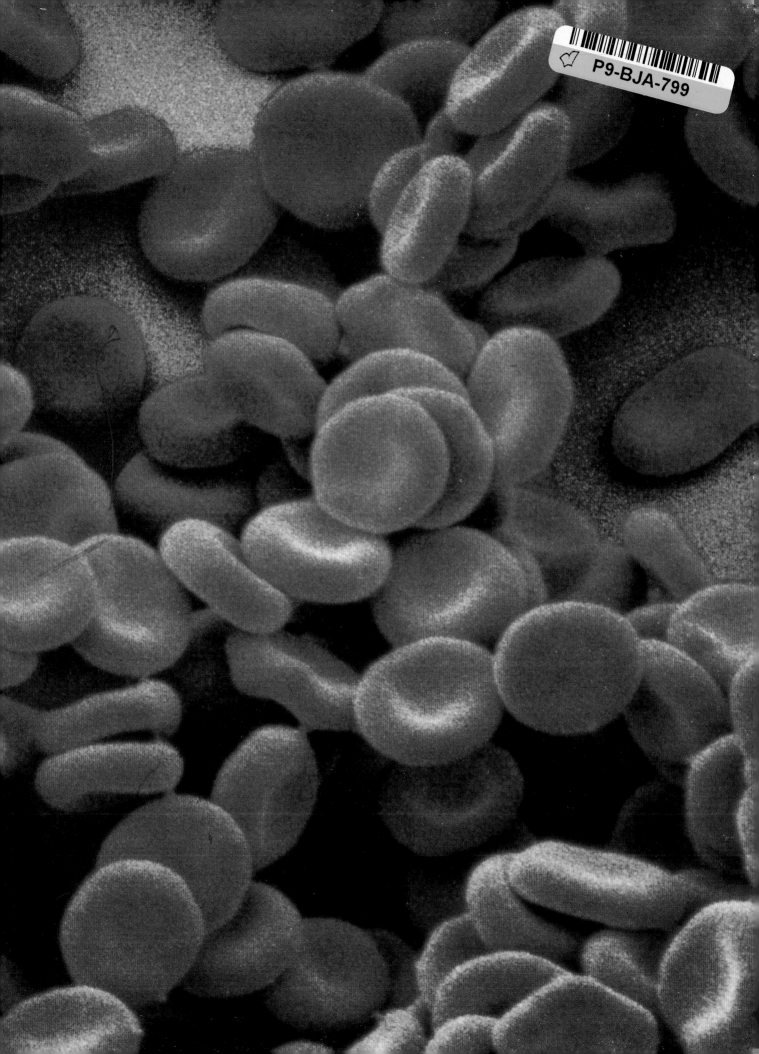

HUMAN BODY

Written by
DR. FRANCES WILLIAMS

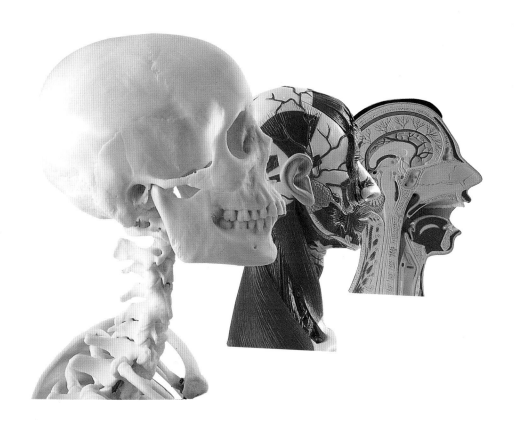

FIREFLY BOOKS

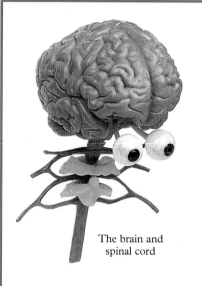

The brain and
spinal cord

A DK PUBLISHING BOOK

Editor Miranda Smith
Art editors Mark Haygarth, Dominic Zwemmer
Photographic art direction Jill Plank
Assistant editor Julie Ferris
DTP designer Nicky Studdart
Managing editor Gillian Denton
Managing art editor Julia Harris
Editorial consultant Dr. Michael Hutchinson
Picture Research James Clarke
Production Charlotte Traill
Photography Geoff Brightling

Handcrafted models by
Denoyer-Geppert, Chicago USA and Bristol UK
Plastic human skeletons by
Educational and Scientific Products Limited UK

First published in Canada in 1997
by Firefly Books Ltd
3680 Victoria Park Avenue
Willowdale, Ontario, M2H 3K1

Canadian Cataloguing in Publication Data

Williams, Frances, Dr.
Human body

(Inside guides)
Includes index.
ISBN 1–55209–116–3

1. Body, Human. 2. Human anatomy.
3. Human physiology. T. Title.

QP38.W54 1997   612   C96 932457–X

Reproduced in Italy by G.R.B. Graphica, Verona
Printed in Singapore by Toppan

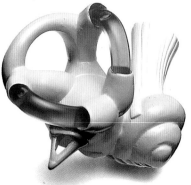

The inner ear

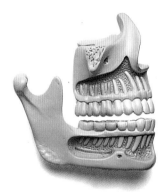

Adult teeth

Cutaway model
of a kidney

Heart and
lungs

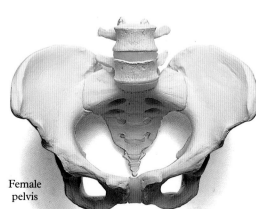

Female
pelvis

Ligamented
knee joint

Composition
of a bone

Contents

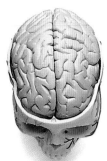

The brain
inside the skull

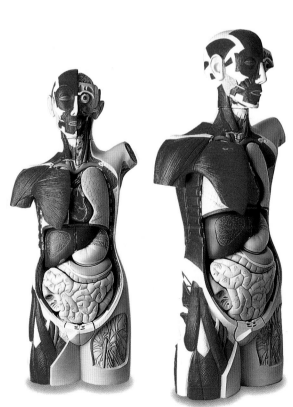

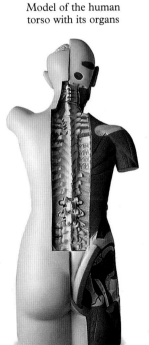

Model of the human
torso with its organs

The body's systems

The human body is a complex collection of millions of individual living units called cells. Different types of similar cells are grouped together to form tissues. Each tissue has its own structure and appearance. Separate body organs, such as the brain and heart, are made up of different tissues. Organs work together in groups known as systems that each have their own important set of functions to perform. All the systems work in close harmony to ensure that the body remains healthy.

Nervous system
The nervous system (pp.16–21) is the body's chief control system. It receives information and sends out instructions through nerves to all parts of the body.

Skin, hair, and nails
Skin (pp.36–37) provides the body's covering. Skin is protective, waterproof, and supple enough to allow movement. Skin also senses touch, pressure, and pain, and helps control the temperature of the body. Hair and nails grow from the skin.

Cardiovascular system
The cardiovascular system, or heart and circulation (pp.22–25), is the body's transport system. The heart pumps blood, which circulates around the body. Blood distributes oxygen, nutrients, and other substances.

Sensory system
The sensory system is part of the nervous system which relays information about the body to the brain. The information is collected by detectors called sensory receptors. Taste, smell, sight, and sound (pp.32–35) are special senses.

Muscular system
Contraction of muscles (pp.14–15) attached to bones causes movement of the skeleton. Skeletal muscles give the body much of its bulk. The heart contains a type of muscle called cardiac muscle. Other internal organs contain a type called smooth muscle.

Respiratory system
This system (pp.26–27) carries air into and out of the lungs. In the lungs, oxygen passes into the blood and carbon dioxide passes out.

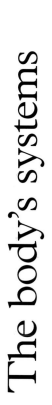

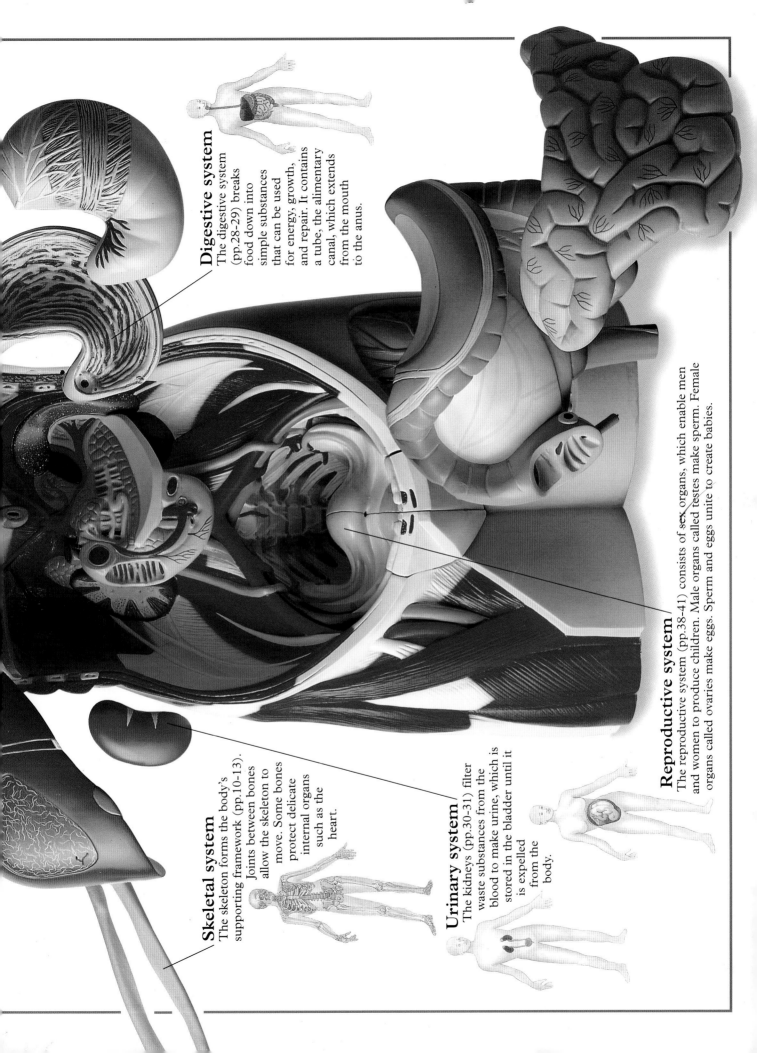

Digestive system
The digestive system (pp.28-29) breaks food down into simple substances that can be used for energy, growth, and repair. It contains a tube, the alimentary canal, which extends from the mouth to the anus.

Reproductive system
The reproductive system (pp.38-41) consists of sex organs, which enable men and women to produce children. Male organs called testes make sperm. Female organs called ovaries make eggs. Sperm and eggs unite to create babies.

Skeletal system
The skeleton forms the body's supporting framework (pp.10-13). Joints between bones allow the skeleton to move. Some bones protect delicate internal organs such as the heart.

Urinary system
The kidneys (pp.30-31) filter waste substances from the blood to make urine, which is stored in the bladder until it is expelled from the body.

The skeleton

The skeleton is the strong inner framework of the body. It is made up of separate bones, linked together by joints. Your skeleton gives your body shape and supports and protects important organs, such as the brain and heart. Although each bone is rigid, the skeleton can move because the joints between bones are flexible. Before birth, the skeleton is somewhat soft because it is made of cartilage (gristle). Cartilage gradually changes into hard bone as your body grows.

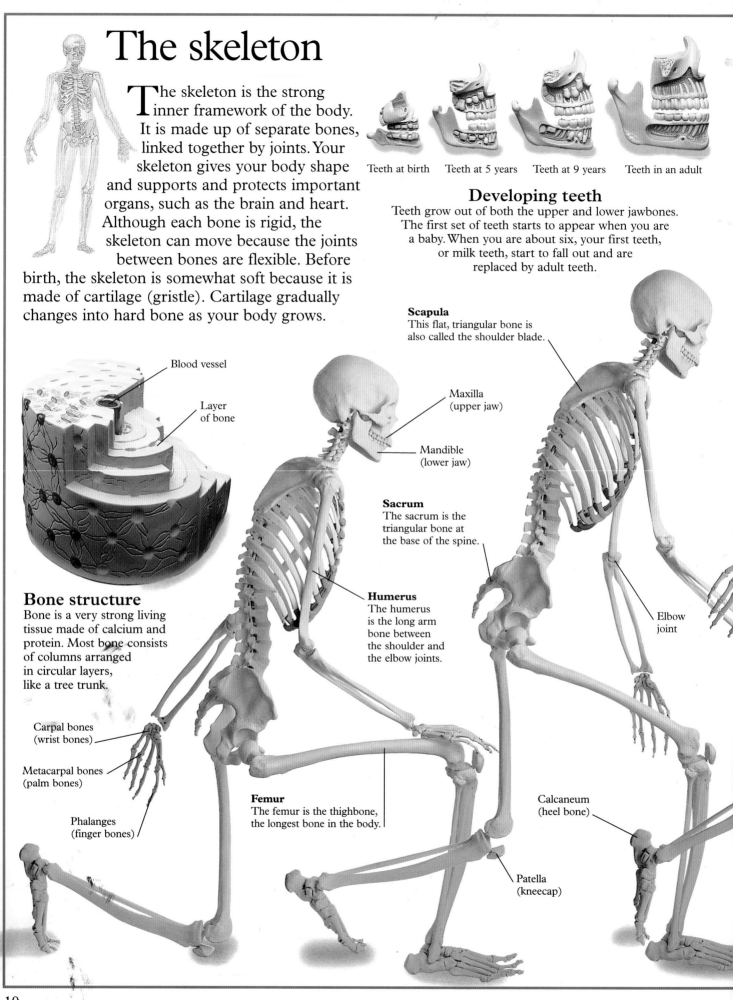

Teeth at birth   Teeth at 5 years   Teeth at 9 years   Teeth in an adult

Developing teeth
Teeth grow out of both the upper and lower jawbones. The first set of teeth starts to appear when you are a baby. When you are about six, your first teeth, or milk teeth, start to fall out and are replaced by adult teeth.

Scapula
This flat, triangular bone is also called the shoulder blade.

Maxilla
(upper jaw)

Mandible
(lower jaw)

Sacrum
The sacrum is the triangular bone at the base of the spine.

Humerus
The humerus is the long arm bone between the shoulder and the elbow joints.

Elbow
joint

Blood vessel

Layer
of bone

Bone structure
Bone is a very strong living tissue made of calcium and protein. Most bone consists of columns arranged in circular layers, like a tree trunk.

Carpal bones
(wrist bones)

Metacarpal bones
(palm bones)

Phalanges
(finger bones)

Femur
The femur is the thighbone, the longest bone in the body.

Calcaneum
(heel bone)

Patella
(kneecap)

Bones of the body

The skeleton is made up of about 200 separate bones. Each bone has its own name and shape. The skull, spine, ribs, and breastbone form the central part of the skeleton. The bones of the arms, shoulders, legs, and hips hang symmetrically on each side.

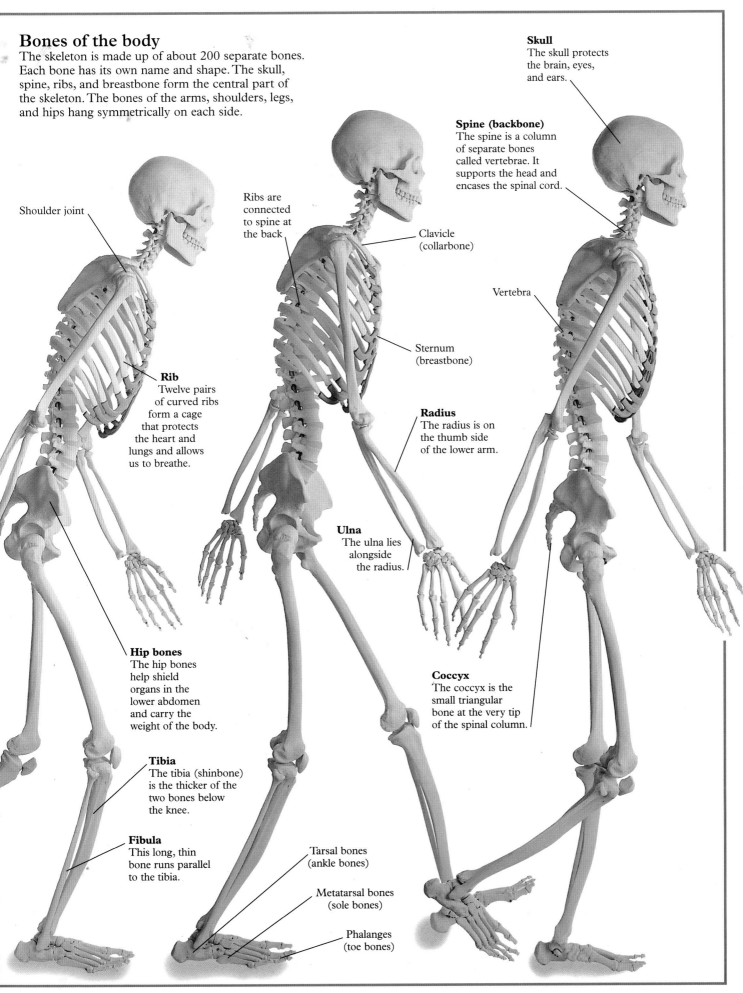

Skull
The skull protects the brain, eyes, and ears.

Spine (backbone)
The spine is a column of separate bones called vertebrae. It supports the head and encases the spinal cord.

Shoulder joint

Ribs are connected to spine at the back

Clavicle (collarbone)

Vertebra

Sternum (breastbone)

Rib
Twelve pairs of curved ribs form a cage that protects the heart and lungs and allows us to breathe.

Radius
The radius is on the thumb side of the lower arm.

Ulna
The ulna lies alongside the radius.

Hip bones
The hip bones help shield organs in the lower abdomen and carry the weight of the body.

Coccyx
The coccyx is the small triangular bone at the very tip of the spinal column.

Tibia
The tibia (shinbone) is the thicker of the two bones below the knee.

Fibula
This long, thin bone runs parallel to the tibia.

Tarsal bones (ankle bones)

Metatarsal bones (sole bones)

Phalanges (toe bones)

11

Joints and movement

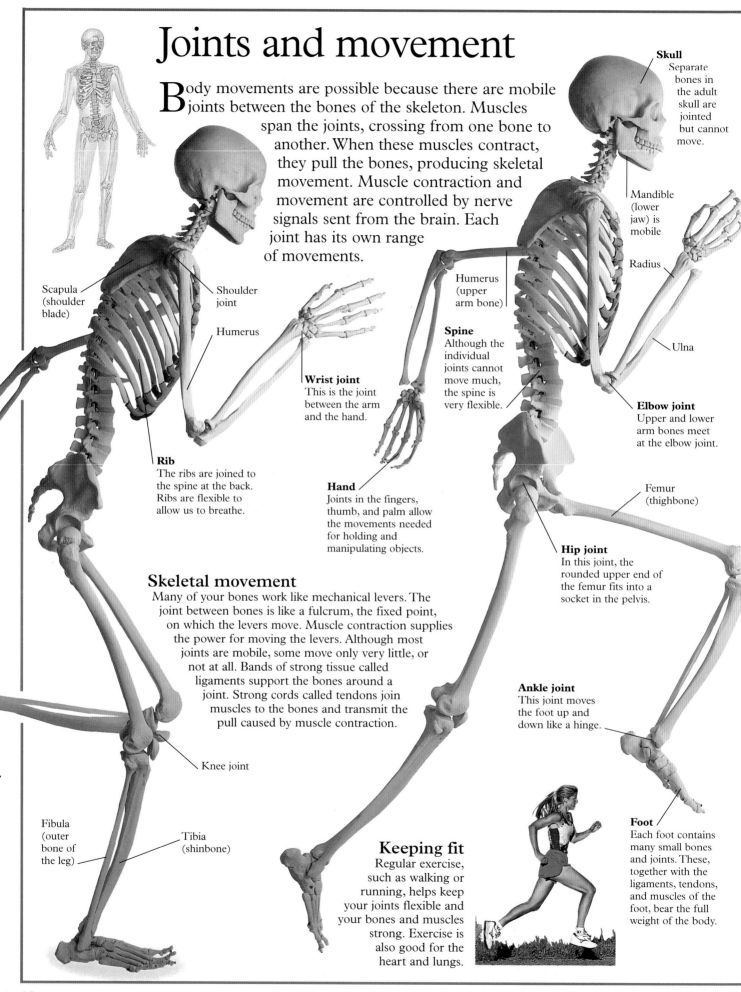

Body movements are possible because there are mobile joints between the bones of the skeleton. Muscles span the joints, crossing from one bone to another. When these muscles contract, they pull the bones, producing skeletal movement. Muscle contraction and movement are controlled by nerve signals sent from the brain. Each joint has its own range of movements.

Skull
Separate bones in the adult skull are jointed but cannot move.

Mandible (lower jaw) is mobile

Radius

Humerus (upper arm bone)

Ulna

Spine
Although the individual joints cannot move much, the spine is very flexible.

Elbow joint
Upper and lower arm bones meet at the elbow joint.

Scapula (shoulder blade)

Shoulder joint

Humerus

Wrist joint
This is the joint between the arm and the hand.

Rib
The ribs are joined to the spine at the back. Ribs are flexible to allow us to breathe.

Hand
Joints in the fingers, thumb, and palm allow the movements needed for holding and manipulating objects.

Femur (thighbone)

Hip joint
In this joint, the rounded upper end of the femur fits into a socket in the pelvis.

Skeletal movement
Many of your bones work like mechanical levers. The joint between bones is like a fulcrum, the fixed point, on which the levers move. Muscle contraction supplies the power for moving the levers. Although most joints are mobile, some move only very little, or not at all. Bands of strong tissue called ligaments support the bones around a joint. Strong cords called tendons join muscles to the bones and transmit the pull caused by muscle contraction.

Ankle joint
This joint moves the foot up and down like a hinge.

Knee joint

Fibula (outer bone of the leg)

Tibia (shinbone)

Keeping fit
Regular exercise, such as walking or running, helps keep your joints flexible and your bones and muscles strong. Exercise is also good for the heart and lungs.

Foot
Each foot contains many small bones and joints. These, together with the ligaments, tendons, and muscles of the foot, bear the full weight of the body.

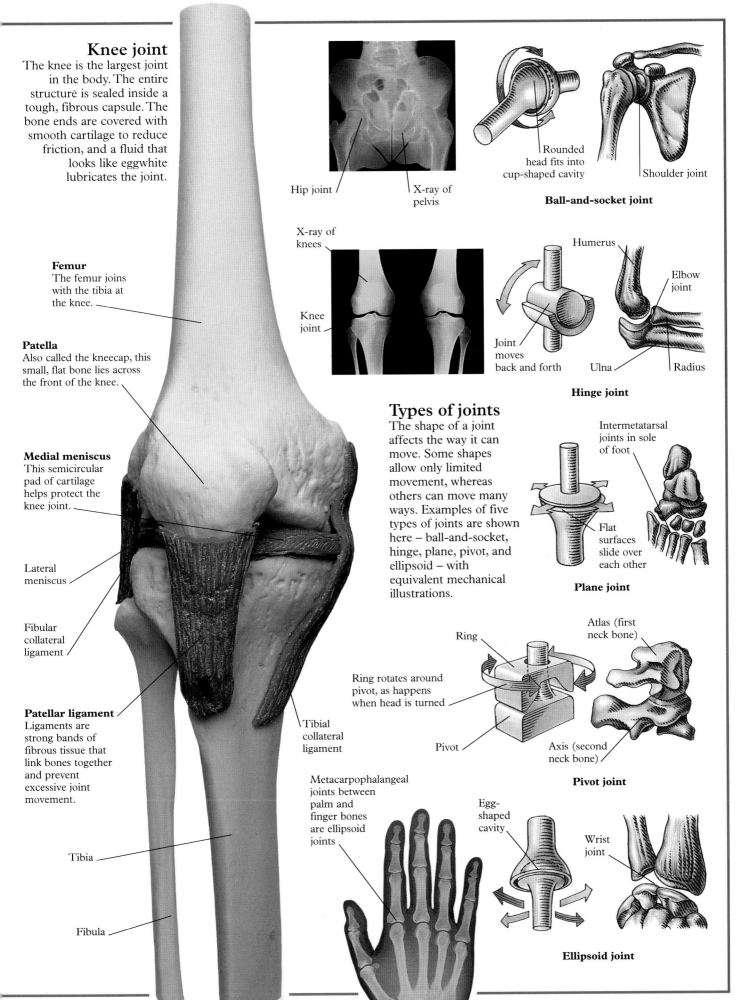

Knee joint

The knee is the largest joint in the body. The entire structure is sealed inside a tough, fibrous capsule. The bone ends are covered with smooth cartilage to reduce friction, and a fluid that looks like eggwhite lubricates the joint.

Femur
The femur joins with the tibia at the knee.

Patella
Also called the kneecap, this small, flat bone lies across the front of the knee.

Medial meniscus
This semicircular pad of cartilage helps protect the knee joint.

Lateral meniscus

Fibular collateral ligament

Patellar ligament
Ligaments are strong bands of fibrous tissue that link bones together and prevent excessive joint movement.

Tibia

Fibula

Tibial collateral ligament

Hip joint

X-ray of pelvis

Rounded head fits into cup-shaped cavity

Shoulder joint

Ball-and-socket joint

X-ray of knees

Knee joint

Humerus

Elbow joint

Joint moves back and forth

Ulna

Radius

Hinge joint

Types of joints

The shape of a joint affects the way it can move. Some shapes allow only limited movement, whereas others can move many ways. Examples of five types of joints are shown here – ball-and-socket, hinge, plane, pivot, and ellipsoid – with equivalent mechanical illustrations.

Intermetatarsal joints in sole of foot

Flat surfaces slide over each other

Plane joint

Ring

Ring rotates around pivot, as happens when head is turned

Pivot

Atlas (first neck bone)

Axis (second neck bone)

Pivot joint

Metacarpophalangeal joints between palm and finger bones are ellipsoid joints

Egg-shaped cavity

Wrist joint

Ellipsoid joint

13

Body muscles

Muscles produce every movement your body makes. They are made of thin fibers that can contract to make part of your body move or change shape. There are three types of muscles in the body. Cardiac muscle is present only in the heart, and smooth muscle is located in the walls of the intestines, bladder, and other internal organs. However, skeletal muscle is the main type of muscle. It is attached to the skeleton and makes the bones move. Many skeletal muscles are connected to bone by tough cords called tendons. There are hundreds of different skeletal muscles. Each muscle is a different size and shape, and each has its own function.

Lowering forearm

Triceps contracts

Elbow straightens

Upper arm

Forearm

Raising forearm

Biceps contracts

Elbow bends

Moving the forearm
When you lower your forearm, the triceps muscle at the back of your upper arm contracts and your elbow straightens. When you raise your forearm, the biceps muscle at the front of your upper arm contracts and your elbow bends.

Head and neck muscles
Powerful muscles in the head move your jaw and bring your teeth together for chewing. Other head muscles move your eyes, cheeks, and mouth. Strong muscles in the neck move the head and keep it upright.

Temporalis
This muscle closes the mouth and clenches the teeth.

Frontalis
The frontalis muscle raises the eyebrows and wrinkles the forehead.

Orbicularis oculi
This encircles the eye and closes the eyelids.

Occipitalis pulls scalp backward

Trapezius

Orbicularis oris
This surrounds the opening of the mouth.

Buccinator
This muscle presses the cheeks against your teeth when you eat, and also blows air out of the mouth.

Sternocleidomastoid
This muscle pulls the head forward and turns or tilts it to the side.

Facial expressions
Muscles around the eyes, nose, and mouth control expressions of the face. They make you frown when you are annoyed, smile when happy, and raise your eyebrows when surprised.

Frontalis

Sternocleidomastoid

Scapula
(shoulder blade)

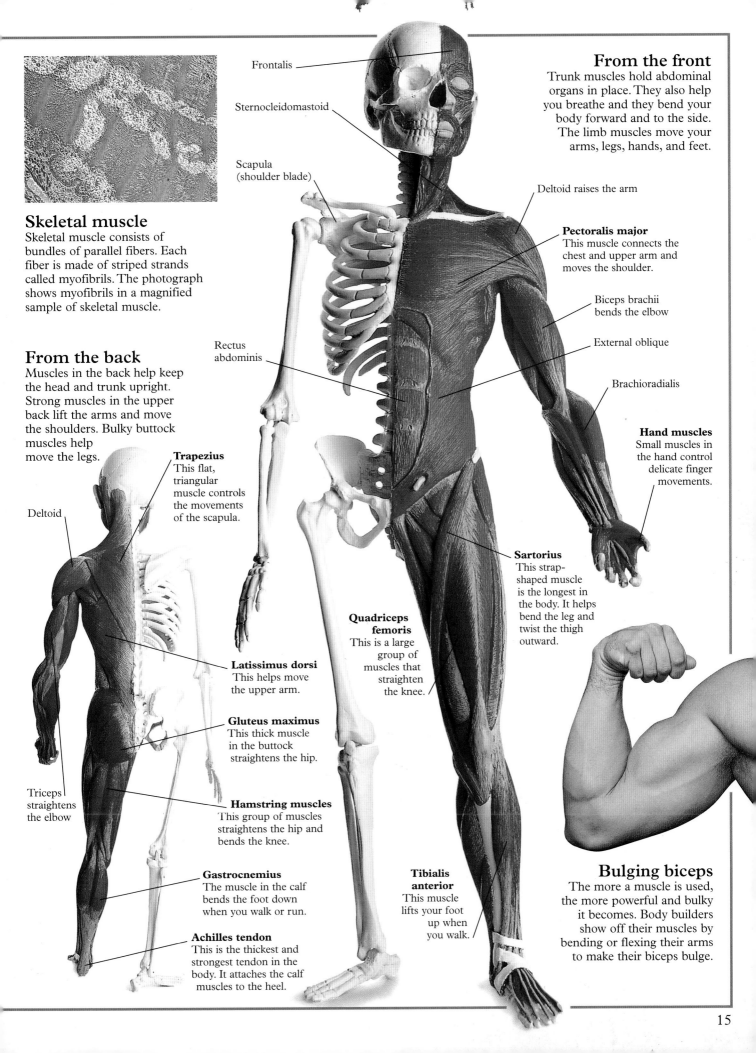

Skeletal muscle
Skeletal muscle consists of
bundles of parallel fibers. Each
fiber is made of striped strands
called myofibrils. The photograph
shows myofibrils in a magnified
sample of skeletal muscle.

From the back
Muscles in the back help keep
the head and trunk upright.
Strong muscles in the upper
back lift the arms and move
the shoulders. Bulky buttock
muscles help
move the legs.

Deltoid

Triceps
straightens
the elbow

Rectus
abdominis

Trapezius
This flat,
triangular
muscle controls
the movements
of the scapula.

Latissimus dorsi
This helps move
the upper arm.

Gluteus maximus
This thick muscle
in the buttock
straightens the hip.

Hamstring muscles
This group of muscles
straightens the hip and
bends the knee.

Gastrocnemius
The muscle in the calf
bends the foot down
when you walk or run.

Achilles tendon
This is the thickest and
strongest tendon in the
body. It attaches the calf
muscles to the heel.

**Quadriceps
femoris**
This is a large
group of
muscles that
straighten
the knee.

**Tibialis
anterior**
This muscle
lifts your foot
up when
you walk.

From the front
Trunk muscles hold abdominal
organs in place. They also help
you breathe and they bend your
body forward and to the side.
The limb muscles move your
arms, legs, hands, and feet.

Deltoid raises the arm

Pectoralis major
This muscle connects the
chest and upper arm and
moves the shoulder.

Biceps brachii
bends the elbow

External oblique

Brachioradialis

Hand muscles
Small muscles in
the hand control
delicate finger
movements.

Sartorius
This strap-
shaped muscle
is the longest in
the body. It helps
bend the leg and
twist the thigh
outward.

Bulging biceps
The more a muscle is used,
the more powerful and bulky
it becomes. Body builders
show off their muscles by
bending or flexing their arms
to make their biceps bulge.

The head

Your head balances at the top of your trunk, held up by the bones and muscles of your neck. It contains the brain, which is the body's control center. It also contains sense organs that allow you to see, hear, smell, and taste. Your brain and sense organs are protected by a strong case of bone called the skull. The front of your skull is covered by muscles that move your forehead, eyelids, cheeks, mouth, and chin. On top of these muscles lie the features that make your face distinctive.

Under the skin
The muscles under the skin of your face control a huge range of expressions, like smiling and frowning. Powerful muscles move the jaw when chewing and help keep the head upright. The top of the head is covered by a tough layer of skin called the scalp.

The scalp
The skin of the scalp contains thousands of tiny holes called follicles from which hairs can grow.

Frontalis muscle
The frontalis muscle helps wrinkle the forehead and raise the eyebrows.

Orbicularis oculi muscle
This circular muscle around each eye tightens briefly thousands of times each day to blink the eyelid.

Lips
The lips are soft folds around the mouth. They keep food inside the mouth and help produce sounds.

Orbicularis oris muscle
This muscle surrounds the opening of the mouth. It closes your lips and helps you speak and eat.

Zygomatic bone
This prominent bone is also called the cheekbone.

The maxilla or upper jaw

Temporalis muscle
This muscle helps lift the lower jaw and closes the mouth.

Cheek muscles

Masseter muscle
This muscle helps lift the lower jaw and brings the teeth together for chewing.

Neck muscles
These help hold the head upright and also control the bending and twisting of the neck.

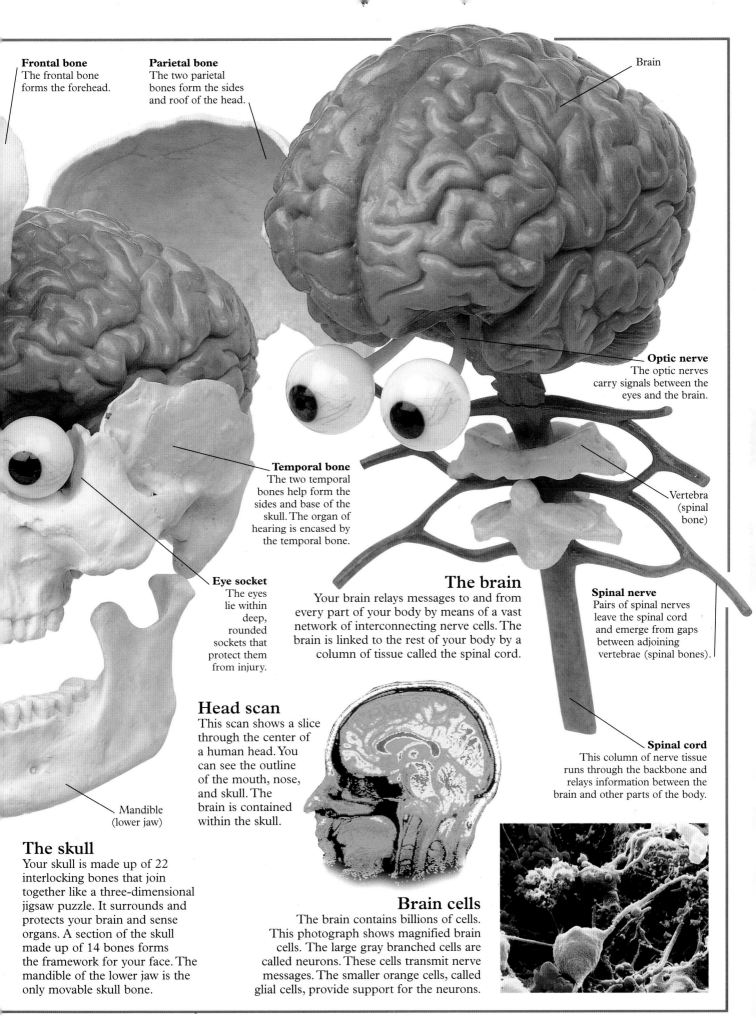

Frontal bone
The frontal bone forms the forehead.

Parietal bone
The two parietal bones form the sides and roof of the head.

Brain

Optic nerve
The optic nerves carry signals between the eyes and the brain.

Temporal bone
The two temporal bones help form the sides and base of the skull. The organ of hearing is encased by the temporal bone.

Vertebra (spinal bone)

Eye socket
The eyes lie within deep, rounded sockets that protect them from injury.

The brain
Your brain relays messages to and from every part of your body by means of a vast network of interconnecting nerve cells. The brain is linked to the rest of your body by a column of tissue called the spinal cord.

Spinal nerve
Pairs of spinal nerves leave the spinal cord and emerge from gaps between adjoining vertebrae (spinal bones).

Head scan
This scan shows a slice through the center of a human head. You can see the outline of the mouth, nose, and skull. The brain is contained within the skull.

Mandible (lower jaw)

Spinal cord
This column of nerve tissue runs through the backbone and relays information between the brain and other parts of the body.

The skull
Your skull is made up of 22 interlocking bones that join together like a three-dimensional jigsaw puzzle. It surrounds and protects your brain and sense organs. A section of the skull made up of 14 bones forms the framework for your face. The mandible of the lower jaw is the only movable skull bone.

Brain cells
The brain contains billions of cells. This photograph shows magnified brain cells. The large gray branched cells are called neurons. These cells transmit nerve messages. The smaller orange cells, called glial cells, provide support for the neurons.

The brain

The brain is the control center of all your body's activities. It relays messages to and from every part of the body through the spinal cord and nerves. Your brain enables you to move, speak, sense, think, feel, understand, learn, and remember. It also regulates automatic functions that keep you alive, like the beating of your heart and breathing. The brain has a very complicated structure, organized into many different parts, each with its own job. The brain of an adult weighs about 3 lb (1.4 kg).

Right cerebral hemisphere

Left cerebral hemisphere

From the top
The largest part of the brain is called the cerebrum. It resembles a large wrinkled walnut. It is divided into two halves called cerebral hemispheres.

Roof of skull lifted

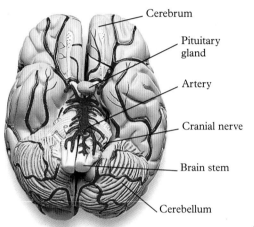

Cerebrum

Pituitary gland

Artery

Cranial nerve

Brain stem

Cerebellum

Base of the brain
Arteries running over the surface of the brain keep it well supplied with blood and oxygen at all times. Twelve pairs of nerves, called cranial nerves, branch directly from the base of the brain.

Cerebrum
The cerebrum forms the bulk of the brain. It deals with our conscious thoughts, movements, and sensations.

Left cerebral hemisphere

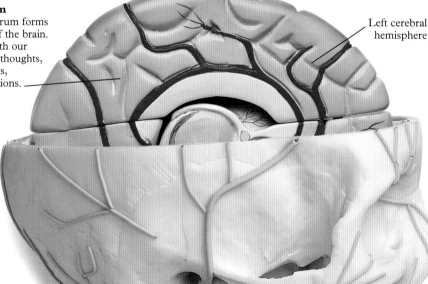

Neurocranium

Brain box
The brain is safely protected inside the head by the skull. The part of the skull that encloses the brain is called the neurocranium, and the remainder of the skull is called the facial skeleton. Lifting the roof of the skull reveals the brain inside.

Facial skeleton
The skull forms the framework of the face. The face is made up of 14 bones. The jaw contains sockets for the teeth.

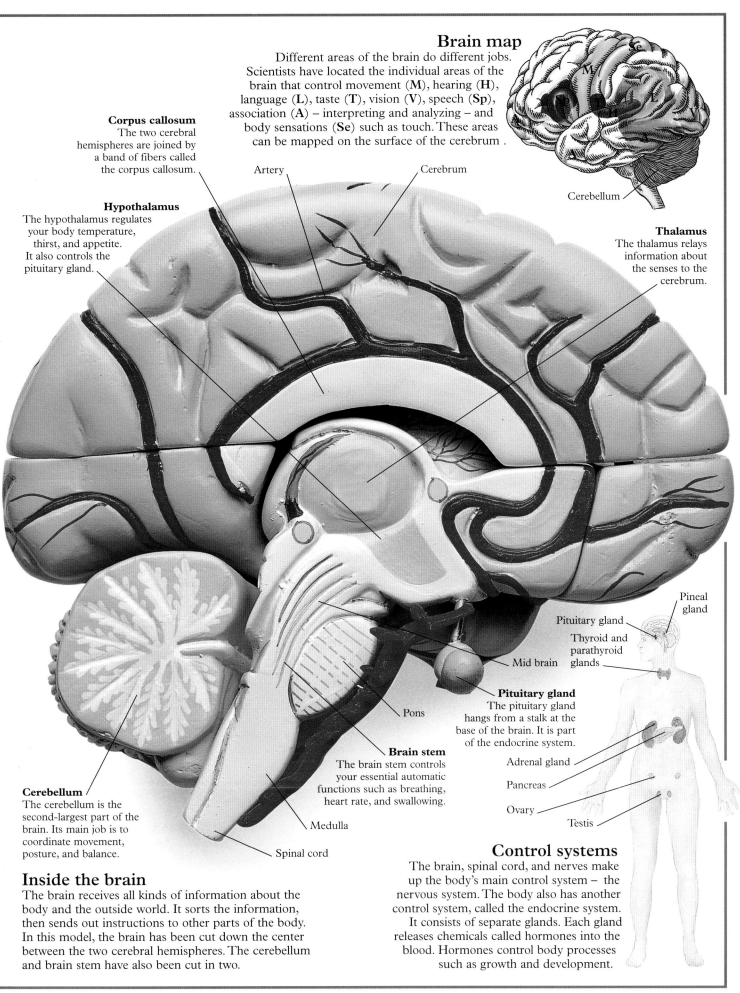

Brain map
Different areas of the brain do different jobs. Scientists have located the individual areas of the brain that control movement (**M**), hearing (**H**), language (**L**), taste (**T**), vision (**V**), speech (**Sp**), association (**A**) – interpreting and analyzing – and body sensations (**Se**) such as touch. These areas can be mapped on the surface of the cerebrum .

Cerebellum

Corpus callosum
The two cerebral hemispheres are joined by a band of fibers called the corpus callosum.

Artery

Cerebrum

Hypothalamus
The hypothalamus regulates your body temperature, thirst, and appetite. It also controls the pituitary gland.

Thalamus
The thalamus relays information about the senses to the cerebrum.

Pineal gland

Pituitary gland

Thyroid and parathyroid glands

Mid brain

Pons

Pituitary gland
The pituitary gland hangs from a stalk at the base of the brain. It is part of the endocrine system.

Adrenal gland

Pancreas

Brain stem
The brain stem controls your essential automatic functions such as breathing, heart rate, and swallowing.

Ovary

Testis

Cerebellum
The cerebellum is the second-largest part of the brain. Its main job is to coordinate movement, posture, and balance.

Medulla

Spinal cord

Inside the brain
The brain receives all kinds of information about the body and the outside world. It sorts the information, then sends out instructions to other parts of the body. In this model, the brain has been cut down the center between the two cerebral hemispheres. The cerebellum and brain stem have also been cut in two.

Control systems
The brain, spinal cord, and nerves make up the body's main control system – the nervous system. The body also has another control system, called the endocrine system. It consists of separate glands. Each gland releases chemicals called hormones into the blood. Hormones control body processes such as growth and development.

19

The nervous system

The nervous system is controlled by the brain, which is linked with the whole body through the spinal cord and a system of branching nerves. The nervous system contains billions of nerve cells called neurons. Sensory neurons relay messages about sensations toward the brain. Motor neurons relay messages away from the brain to control movements. If you touch something hot, pain triggers a signal that passes along sensory neurons to your spinal cord. The signal passes to motor neurons, which carries it to your muscles to make them contract. This causes you to lift up your hand in a split-second reaction called a reflex.

Spinal nerves
The spinal cord passes from the brain through a tunnel in the spine (backbone). Pairs of spinal nerves emerge from either side of the spinal cord. The spine is divided into cervical, thoracic, lumbar, and sacral parts.

Vertebra
The separate bones in the spine are called vertebrae.

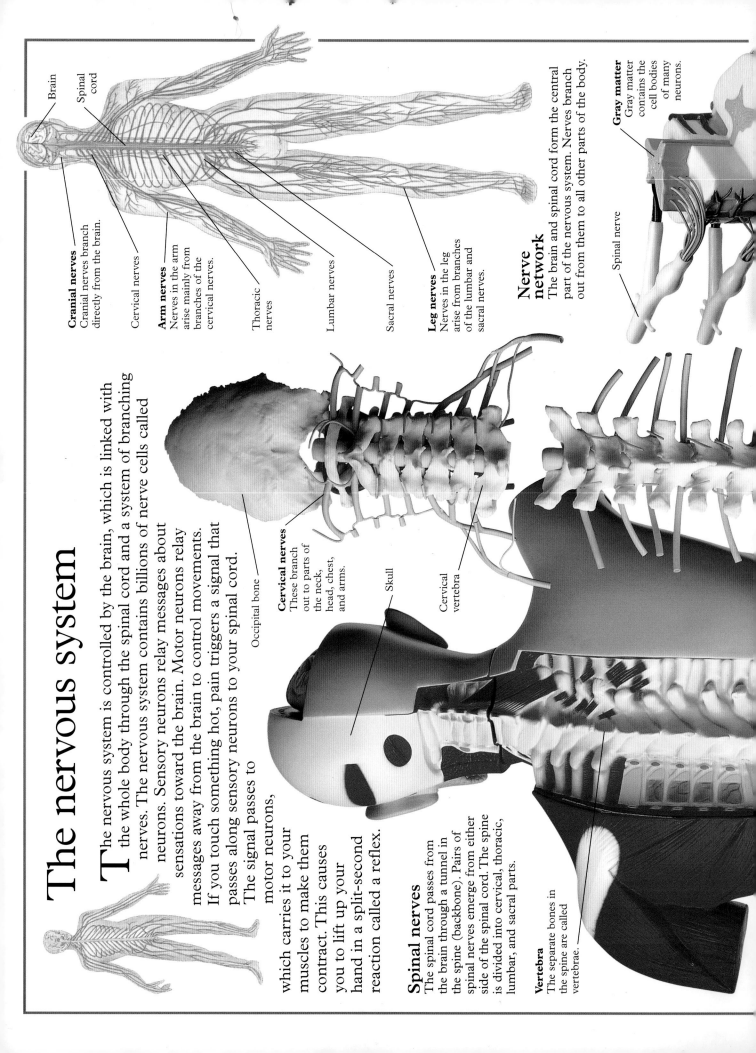

Brain

Spinal cord

Cranial nerves
Cranial nerves branch directly from the brain.

Cervical nerves

Arm nerves
Nerves in the arm arise mainly from branches of the cervical nerves.

Thoracic nerves

Lumbar nerves

Sacral nerves

Leg nerves
Nerves in the leg arise from branches of the lumbar and sacral nerves.

Nerve network
The brain and spinal cord form the central part of the nervous system. Nerves branch out from them to all other parts of the body.

Gray matter
Gray matter contains the cell bodies of many neurons.

Spinal nerve

Cervical nerves
These branch out to parts of the neck, head, chest, and arms.

Occipital bone

Skull

Cervical vertebra

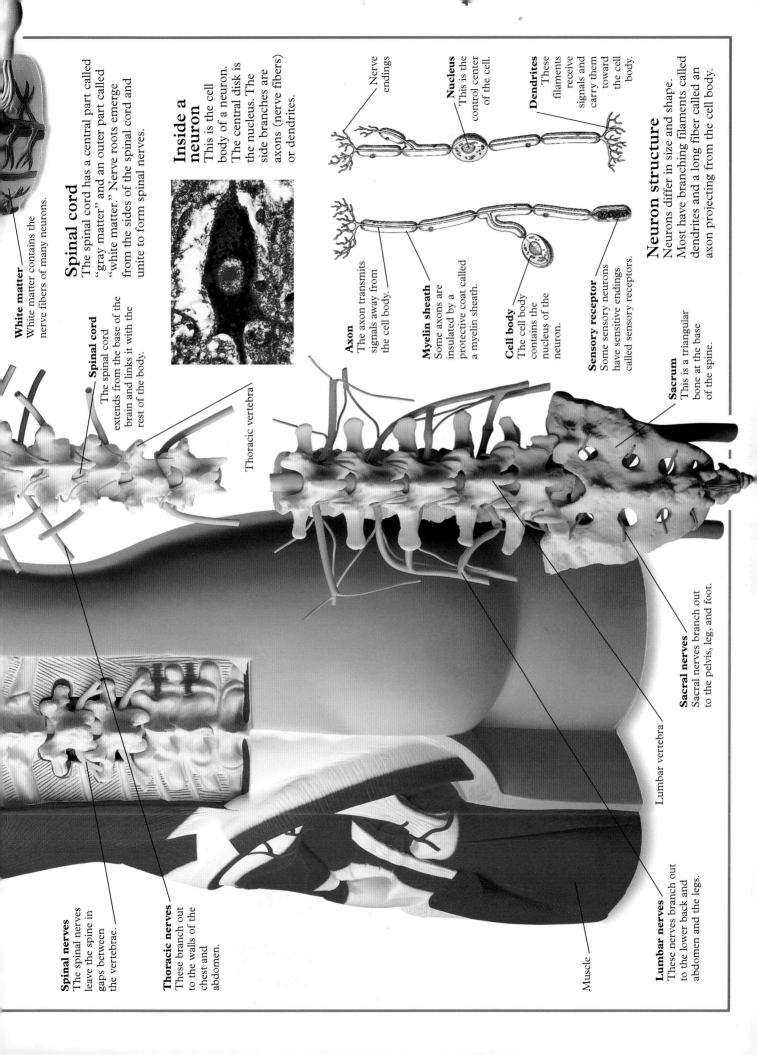

White matter
White matter contains the nerve fibers of many neurons.

Spinal cord
The spinal cord has a central part called "gray matter," and an outer part called "white matter." Nerve roots emerge from the sides of the spinal cord and unite to form spinal nerves.

Spinal cord
The spinal cord extends from the base of the brain and links it with the rest of the body.

Inside a neuron
This is the cell body of a neuron. The central disk is the nucleus. The side branches are axons (nerve fibers) or dendrites.

Nerve endings

Nucleus
This is the control center of the cell.

Dendrites
These filaments receive signals and carry them toward the cell body.

Neuron structure
Neurons differ in size and shape. Most have branching filaments called dendrites and a long fiber called an axon projecting from the cell body.

Axon
The axon transmits signals away from the cell body.

Myelin sheath
Some axons are insulated by a protective coat called a myelin sheath.

Cell body
The cell body contains the nucleus of the neuron.

Sensory receptor
Some sensory neurons have sensitive endings called sensory receptors.

Sacrum
This is a triangular bone at the base of the spine.

Thoracic vertebra

Lumbar vertebra

Sacral nerves
Sacral nerves branch out to the pelvis, leg, and foot.

Spinal nerves
The spinal nerves leave the spine in gaps between the vertebrae.

Thoracic nerves
These branch out to the walls of the chest and abdomen.

Muscle

Lumbar nerves
These nerves branch out to the lower back and abdomen and the legs.

The heart

Your heart is a powerful muscle that pumps blood to every part of your body. The muscular walls of the heart contract continuously, and each contraction produces a heartbeat that squeezes blood out of the heart's cavity. Blood is pumped into a network of blood vessels called arteries, which carry the blood to the lungs and body tissues. Blood flows back to the heart in another network of blood vessels called veins. Then the process starts again.

Aorta
This large artery carries oxygen-enriched blood away from the heart into the body.

Left atrium

Superior vena cava
This is one of the large veins that bring blood back to the heart from the body.

Right atrium

Checking the pulse
Each heartbeat sends a wave of pressure along your arteries. You can feel the wave as your pulse. This nurse is measuring a patient's pulse rate at the wrist.

Pulmonary trunk
This artery carries blood from the heart to the lungs.

Right ventricle

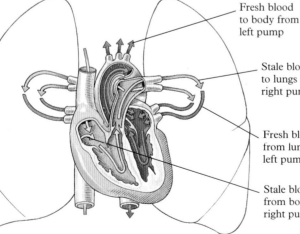

Fresh blood to body from left pump

Stale blood to lungs from right pump

Fresh blood from lungs to left pump

Stale blood from body to right pump

Divided heart
The heart is divided into right and left sides. Each side has an upper chamber called an atrium, and a lower chamber called a ventricle. The thick walls of the ventricles provide the heart's main pumping power.

Left ventricle

Coronary vessels
Coronary arteries and veins provide the blood supply of the heart itself.

Right and left pumps
The left side of the heart pumps fresh, oxygen-rich blood (red) to all body tissues. Stale blood (blue) returns to the right side of the heart, which pumps it to the lungs for more oxygen.

Heartbeats
Tiny electrical signals pass through the heart with each heartbeat. A recording of the signals produces a wavy line called an electrocardiogram, or ECG, which doctors use to check on their patients.

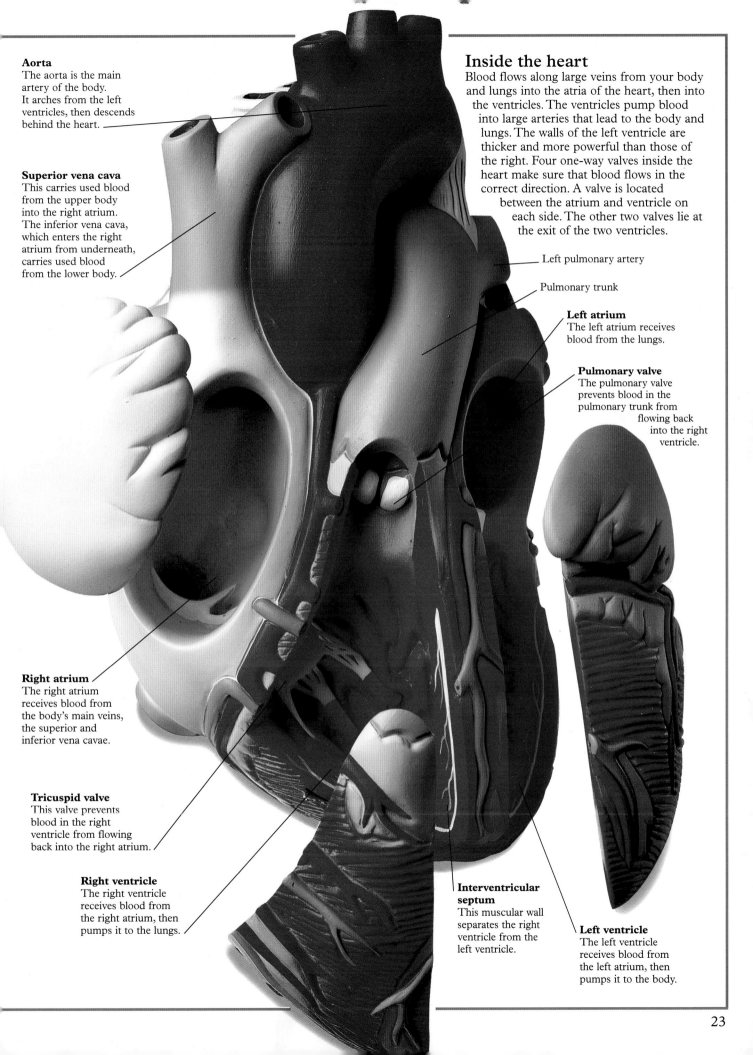

Aorta
The aorta is the main artery of the body. It arches from the left ventricles, then descends behind the heart.

Superior vena cava
This carries used blood from the upper body into the right atrium. The inferior vena cava, which enters the right atrium from underneath, carries used blood from the lower body.

Right atrium
The right atrium receives blood from the body's main veins, the superior and inferior vena cavae.

Tricuspid valve
This valve prevents blood in the right ventricle from flowing back into the right atrium.

Right ventricle
The right ventricle receives blood from the right atrium, then pumps it to the lungs.

Inside the heart

Blood flows along large veins from your body and lungs into the atria of the heart, then into the ventricles. The ventricles pump blood into large arteries that lead to the body and lungs. The walls of the left ventricle are thicker and more powerful than those of the right. Four one-way valves inside the heart make sure that blood flows in the correct direction. A valve is located between the atrium and ventricle on each side. The other two valves lie at the exit of the two ventricles.

Left pulmonary artery

Pulmonary trunk

Left atrium
The left atrium receives blood from the lungs.

Pulmonary valve
The pulmonary valve prevents blood in the pulmonary trunk from flowing back into the right ventricle.

Interventricular septum
This muscular wall separates the right ventricle from the left ventricle.

Left ventricle
The left ventricle receives blood from the left atrium, then pumps it to the body.

23

Blood and circulation

Blood circulates around the body in a system of tubes called blood vessels. The blood and its vessels are the body's transport system. Blood carries oxygen and other vital supplies to all parts of the body and removes carbon dioxide and other harmful wastes. A drop of blood the size of a pinhead contains about six million cells suspended in a watery solution called plasma. The most numerous of these cells are red blood cells. They are shaped like disks and their job is to transport oxygen. White blood cells are larger. They help defend the body against infection. Blood also contains tiny particles called platelets, which help blood clot, preventing too much blood loss from a wound.

Axillary artery

Humerus

Brachial artery

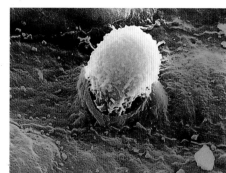

White blood cells
Many white blood cells move out from the blood and travel through other tissues of the body to fight infections. This white blood cell is in the process of passing through the lining of a blood vessel.

Arteries and veins
Fresh blood is pumped from the heart to all body parts along vessels called arteries (red). Used blood returns to the heart in vessels called veins (blue). Running between arteries and veins are smaller blood-carrying vessels called arterioles, capillaries, and venules.

Valve
Veins contain valves that prevent blood from flowing backward.

Elbow veins
Doctors usually take blood samples from a vein at the elbow.

Venous end of capillary

Capillary
The smallest blood vessels are called capillaries.

Smooth muscle cells

Small arteriole
Arterioles divide into smaller branches that lead into a network of capillaries.

Vein
Veins branch into smaller tubes called venules.

Outer layer of vein wall

Thin, muscular layer

Inner coat

Arterial end of capillary

Artery
Arteries branch into smaller vessels called arterioles.

Muscular middle layer of artery wall

Thin, elastic layer

Inner coat

Tough, outer layer

Blood vessels
The walls of arteries are thicker and more muscular than those of veins. Capillaries have very thin walls that allow substances to pass between the blood and the surrounding body cells.

Lymphatic system

The lymphatic system contains a network of lymphatic vessels and lymph nodes. This system drains an excess fluid called lymph from the body tissues back into the blood. It also helps protect against infection.

Lymph duct
Large lymphatic vessels called lymph ducts empty into the blood in the lower neck.

Lymph nodes
Small swellings called lymph nodes are located in clusters along lymphatic vessels.

Lymph nodes in groin

Lymphatic vessels
Lymph is carried from body tissues into the blood in lymphatic vessels.

Spleen
The spleen destroys old red blood cells and helps fight infection.

Intestinal lymphatic vessels
Lymphatic vessels carry digested fats from the intestine.

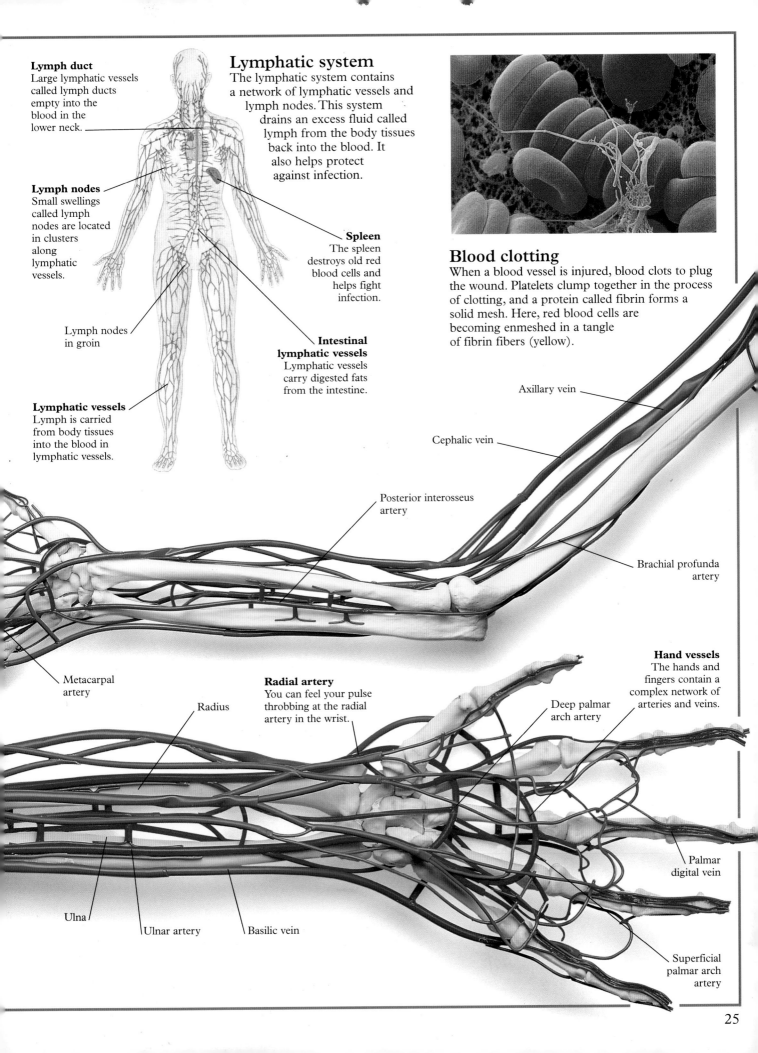

Blood clotting

When a blood vessel is injured, blood clots to plug the wound. Platelets clump together in the process of clotting, and a protein called fibrin forms a solid mesh. Here, red blood cells are becoming enmeshed in a tangle of fibrin fibers (yellow).

Axillary vein

Cephalic vein

Posterior interosseus artery

Brachial profunda artery

Metacarpal artery

Radial artery
You can feel your pulse throbbing at the radial artery in the wrist.

Hand vessels
The hands and fingers contain a complex network of arteries and veins.

Deep palmar arch artery

Palmar digital vein

Radius

Ulna

Ulnar artery

Basilic vein

Superficial palmar arch artery

The respiratory system

To stay alive you need a constant supply of oxygen. You get it by breathing air. When you breathe in, air is drawn in through your nose. The air travels along air passages and enters your lungs. In the lungs, oxygen passes from the air into your blood. At the same time, waste carbon dioxide passes from your blood into the air. You get rid of the carbon dioxide when you breathe out. The entire process is called respiration. The lungs, air passages, and breathing muscles involved make up the respiratory system.

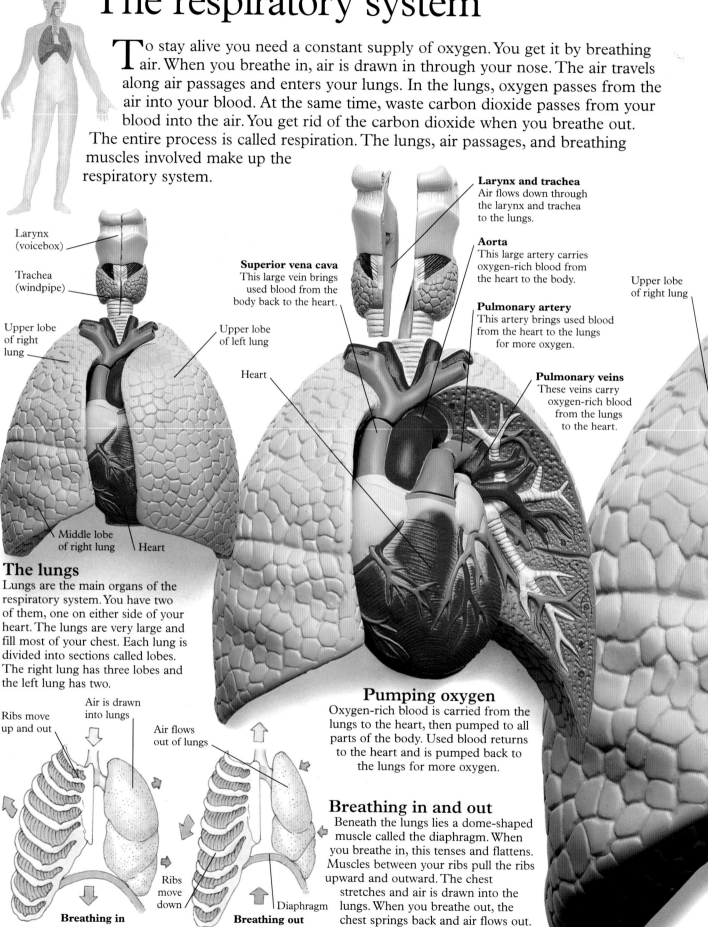

Larynx (voicebox)

Trachea (windpipe)

Upper lobe of right lung

Upper lobe of left lung

Heart

Middle lobe of right lung

Heart

Superior vena cava
This large vein brings used blood from the body back to the heart.

Larynx and trachea
Air flows down through the larynx and trachea to the lungs.

Aorta
This large artery carries oxygen-rich blood from the heart to the body.

Pulmonary artery
This artery brings used blood from the heart to the lungs for more oxygen.

Pulmonary veins
These veins carry oxygen-rich blood from the lungs to the heart.

Upper lobe of right lung

The lungs

Lungs are the main organs of the respiratory system. You have two of them, one on either side of your heart. The lungs are very large and fill most of your chest. Each lung is divided into sections called lobes. The right lung has three lobes and the left lung has two.

Ribs move up and out

Air is drawn into lungs

Air flows out of lungs

Ribs move down

Diaphragm

Breathing in

Breathing out

Pumping oxygen

Oxygen-rich blood is carried from the lungs to the heart, then pumped to all parts of the body. Used blood returns to the heart and is pumped back to the lungs for more oxygen.

Breathing in and out

Beneath the lungs lies a dome-shaped muscle called the diaphragm. When you breathe in, this tenses and flattens. Muscles between your ribs pull the ribs upward and outward. The chest stretches and air is drawn into the lungs. When you breathe out, the chest springs back and air flows out.

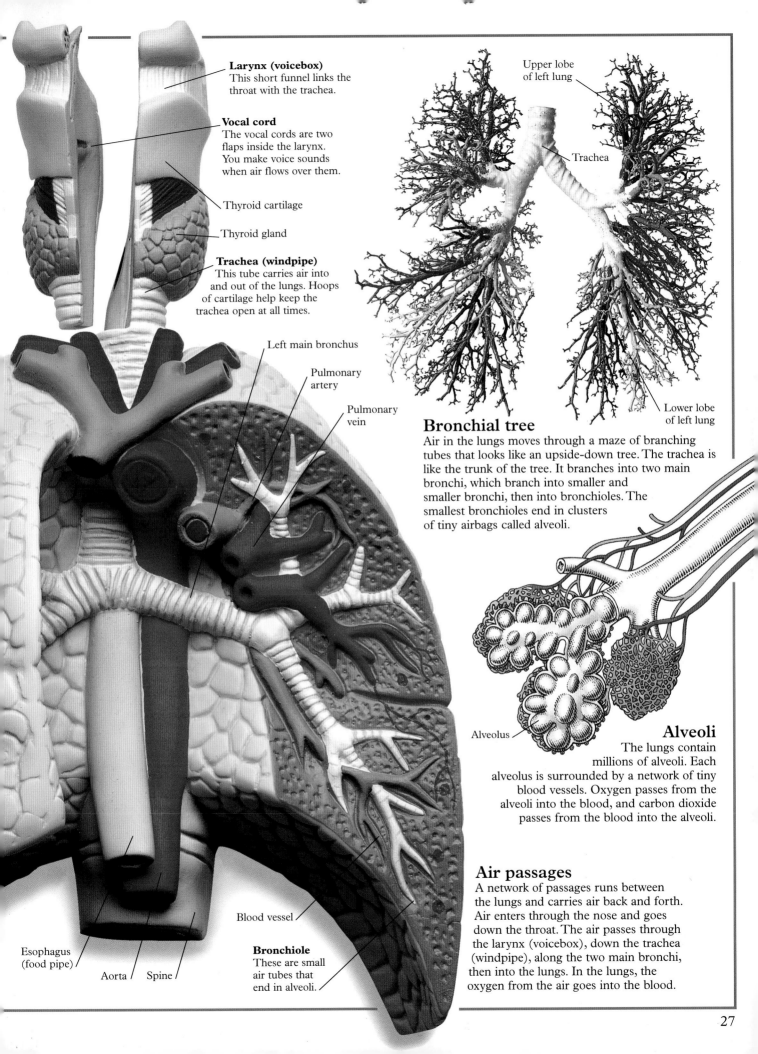

Larynx (voicebox)
This short funnel links the throat with the trachea.

Vocal cord
The vocal cords are two flaps inside the larynx. You make voice sounds when air flows over them.

Thyroid cartilage

Thyroid gland

Trachea (windpipe)
This tube carries air into and out of the lungs. Hoops of cartilage help keep the trachea open at all times.

Left main bronchus

Pulmonary artery

Pulmonary vein

Esophagus (food pipe)

Aorta

Spine

Blood vessel

Bronchiole
These are small air tubes that end in alveoli.

Upper lobe of left lung

Trachea

Lower lobe of left lung

Bronchial tree
Air in the lungs moves through a maze of branching tubes that looks like an upside-down tree. The trachea is like the trunk of the tree. It branches into two main bronchi, which branch into smaller and smaller bronchi, then into bronchioles. The smallest bronchioles end in clusters of tiny airbags called alveoli.

Alveolus

Alveoli
The lungs contain millions of alveoli. Each alveolus is surrounded by a network of tiny blood vessels. Oxygen passes from the alveoli into the blood, and carbon dioxide passes from the blood into the alveoli.

Air passages
A network of passages runs between the lungs and carries air back and forth. Air enters through the nose and goes down the throat. The air passes through the larynx (voicebox), down the trachea (windpipe), along the two main bronchi, then into the lungs. In the lungs, the oxygen from the air goes into the blood.

27

The digestive system

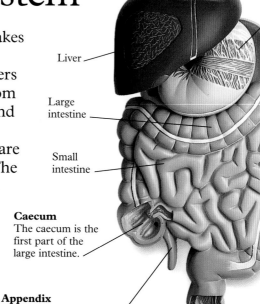

Food provides you with energy, makes you grow, and keeps you healthy. When you eat, the chewed food enters a long, muscular tube that runs from the mouth, through the stomach and intestines, to the anus. Inside the tube, food is broken down into particles that are small enough to pass into your blood. The process of breaking down food is called digestion. Any food that remains undigested passes out of the body as feces through the anus. The liver, gall bladder, and pancreas release fluids that help digest food.

Stomach

Liver

Large intestine

Small intestine

Caecum
The caecum is the first part of the large intestine.

Appendix
The appendix is a short tube that sticks out from the caecum.

Anus

Chewing and swallowing

Digestion begins in the mouth, where food is chewed and mixed with a watery fluid called saliva. Each mouthful is turned into a soft lump that can be easily swallowed. When you swallow, food passes down the throat into a muscular tube called the esophagus. The walls of the esophagus squeeze food down into the stomach.

Organs of digestion

The main digestive organs are the stomach and intestines. The stomach is a hollow bag with muscular walls. It leads into a long, coiled tube called the small intestine, which runs into a wider tube called the large intestine.

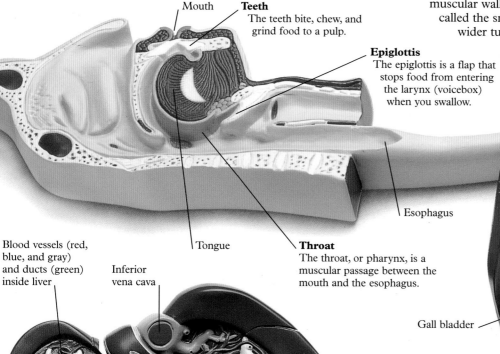

Mouth

Teeth
The teeth bite, chew, and grind food to a pulp.

Epiglottis
The epiglottis is a flap that stops food from entering the larynx (voicebox) when you swallow.

Esophagus

Tongue

Throat
The throat, or pharynx, is a muscular passage between the mouth and the esophagus.

Blood vessels (red, blue, and gray) and ducts (green) inside liver

Inferior vena cava

Gall bladder

The liver

The liver is a large organ located in the upper right part of the abdomen. It makes a fluid called bile that helps digest fatty foods. Bile is stored in a bag called the gall bladder, which nestles underneath the liver.

Gall bladder

Liver
The liver is like a chemical factory. It processes and stores useful substances and gets rid of harmful ones. It also makes a yellowish digestive fluid called bile.

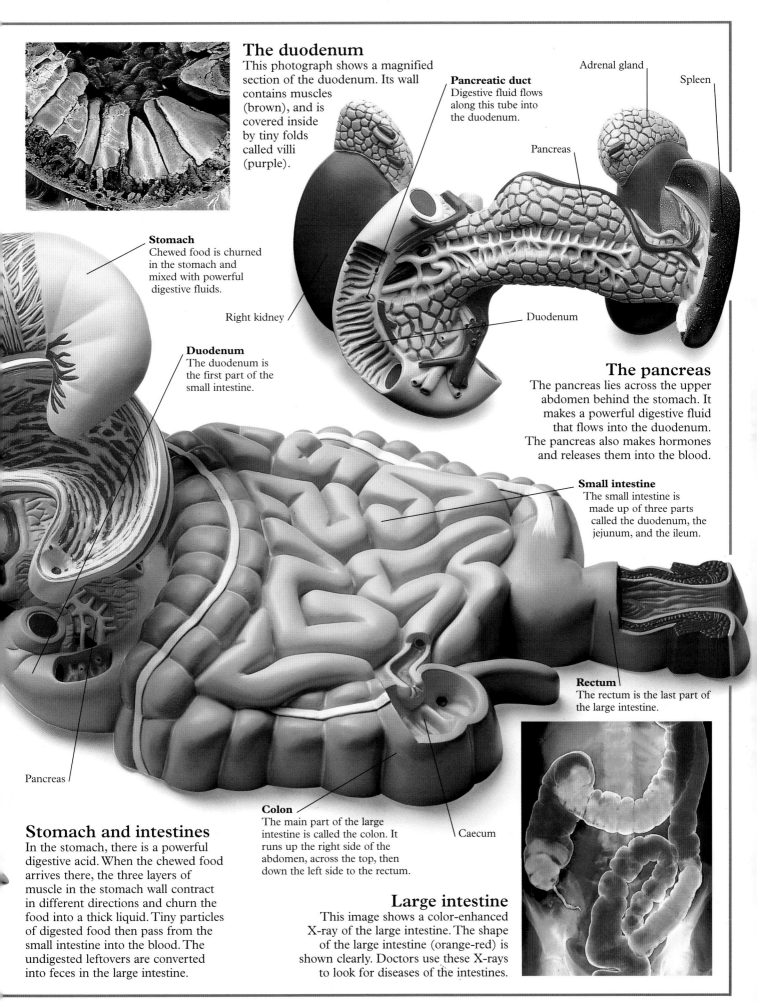

The duodenum
This photograph shows a magnified section of the duodenum. Its wall contains muscles (brown), and is covered inside by tiny folds called villi (purple).

Pancreatic duct
Digestive fluid flows along this tube into the duodenum.

Adrenal gland

Spleen

Pancreas

Duodenum

Stomach
Chewed food is churned in the stomach and mixed with powerful digestive fluids.

Right kidney

Duodenum
The duodenum is the first part of the small intestine.

The pancreas
The pancreas lies across the upper abdomen behind the stomach. It makes a powerful digestive fluid that flows into the duodenum. The pancreas also makes hormones and releases them into the blood.

Small intestine
The small intestine is made up of three parts called the duodenum, the jejunum, and the ileum.

Rectum
The rectum is the last part of the large intestine.

Pancreas

Colon
The main part of the large intestine is called the colon. It runs up the right side of the abdomen, across the top, then down the left side to the rectum.

Caecum

Stomach and intestines
In the stomach, there is a powerful digestive acid. When the chewed food arrives there, the three layers of muscle in the stomach wall contract in different directions and churn the food into a thick liquid. Tiny particles of digested food then pass from the small intestine into the blood. The undigested leftovers are converted into feces in the large intestine.

Large intestine
This image shows a color-enhanced X-ray of the large intestine. The shape of the large intestine (orange-red) is shown clearly. Doctors use these X-rays to look for diseases of the intestines.

The kidneys and bladder

Your kidneys are a pair of bean-shaped organs inside the upper abdomen on either side of the spine. They regulate the fluid inside your body. They also make a watery waste liquid called urine by filtering waste substances and surplus water from the blood. The urine passes from each kidney along two tubes called ureters into a muscular bag called the bladder. When it is time to empty your bladder, the bladder muscle contracts, squeezing the urine out of your body through a tube called the urethra.

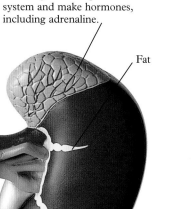

Adrenal gland
This is located above each kidney. The adrenal glands are part of the endocrine system and make hormones, including adrenaline.

Fat

Renal artery
The renal artery brings blood to the kidney.

Renal vein
The renal vein carries blood from the kidney.

Urinary system
The kidneys, bladder, ureters, and urethra together make up the urinary system. While the kidneys make urine, the other organs of the system help remove urine from the body. The kidneys are reddish-brown. The right one is slightly lower than the left in most people.

Left kidney
In adults, each kidney is about 4.4 in (11 cm) long and 2.4 in (6 cm) wide.

Renal pelvis

Aorta (artery)

Inferior vena cava (vein)

Ureter
This muscular tube conveys urine from the kidney to the bladder.

Common iliac artery

Common iliac vein

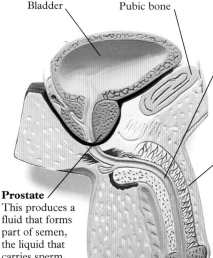

Bladder

Pubic bone

Urethra
In males, the urethra passes through the prostate and along the full length of the penis.

Penis
The penis carries urine out of the body.

Prostate
This produces a fluid that forms part of semen, the liquid that carries sperm.

Scrotum

Prostate
The prostate surrounds the upper part of the urethra in males. As men grow older, the prostate enlarges and can compress the urethra. This may cause problems in emptying the bladder. Females do not have a prostate.

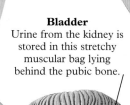

Bladder
Urine from the kidney is stored in this stretchy muscular bag lying behind the pubic bone.

Urethra
A ring of muscle keeps the top tightly shut, except when the bladder is emptying.

Prostate gland

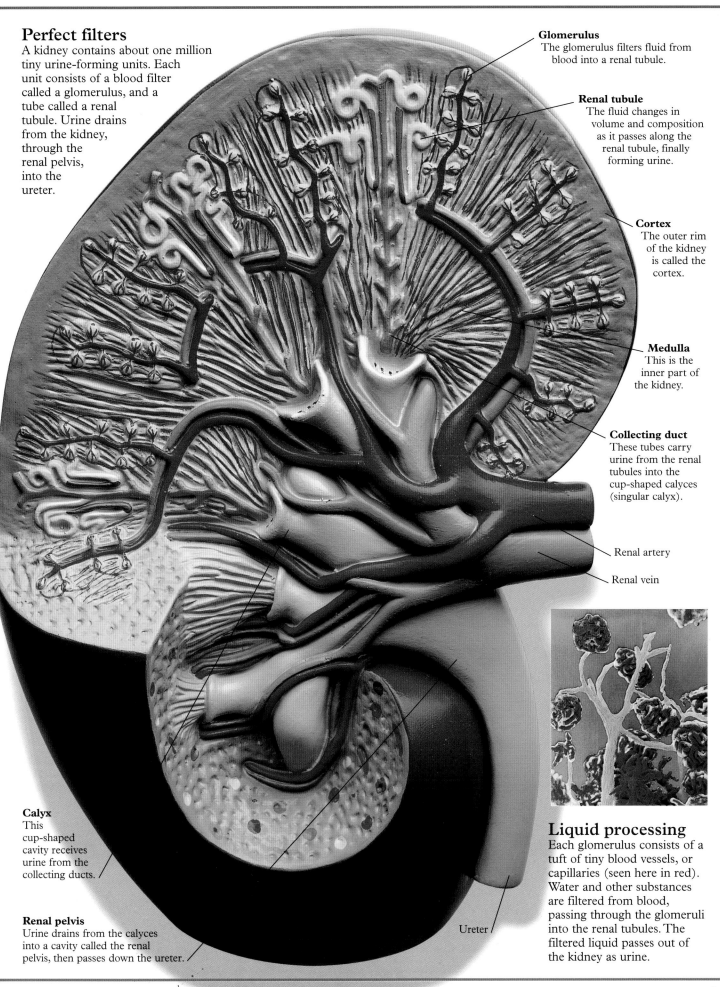

Perfect filters

A kidney contains about one million tiny urine-forming units. Each unit consists of a blood filter called a glomerulus, and a tube called a renal tubule. Urine drains from the kidney, through the renal pelvis, into the ureter.

Glomerulus
The glomerulus filters fluid from blood into a renal tubule.

Renal tubule
The fluid changes in volume and composition as it passes along the renal tubule, finally forming urine.

Cortex
The outer rim of the kidney is called the cortex.

Medulla
This is the inner part of the kidney.

Collecting duct
These tubes carry urine from the renal tubules into the cup-shaped calyces (singular calyx).

Renal artery

Renal vein

Calyx
This cup-shaped cavity receives urine from the collecting ducts.

Renal pelvis
Urine drains from the calyces into a cavity called the renal pelvis, then passes down the ureter.

Ureter

Liquid processing

Each glomerulus consists of a tuft of tiny blood vessels, or capillaries (seen here in red). Water and other substances are filtered from blood, passing through the glomeruli into the renal tubules. The filtered liquid passes out of the kidney as urine.

Taste and smell

The senses of taste and smell are closely related. Together, they help you recognize the various flavors of food and drink. When you have a cold, food may seem less tasty because your sense of smell is impaired. Taste is detected by receptor cells called taste buds located mainly on the tongue. Taste buds are stimulated by substances dissolved in saliva in the mouth. Smell is detected by special nerve endings called olfactory receptor cells in the nose. Olfactory receptor cells are stimulated by airborne substances dissolved in nasal mucus. Messages pass from taste and smell receptor cells along nerves to the brain.

Organ of smell

When you smell, olfactory receptor cells trigger nerve impulses that travel up through tiny holes in the skull bone above the nose. The impulses pass to the olfactory bulbs, then along the olfactory tracts to the brain.

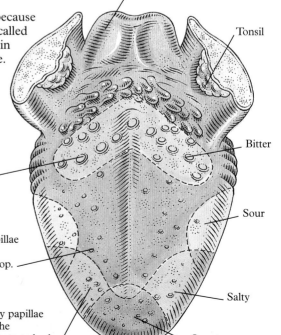

Olfactory bulb
Olfactory nerve impulses from the nose pass to the olfactory bulb, which relays impulses to the brain.

Olfactory tract

Nostril

Nasal cavity
The space inside the nose is lined by a mucus-producing membrane. Mucus production increases when you have a cold.

Olfactory nerves
These nerves carry smell signals from the olfactory membrane.

Olfactory membrane
The roof of the nasal cavity is lined by this moist, sensitive membrane, which contains olfactory receptor cells.

A sense of smell

Protruding from the end of each olfactory receptor cell are 10 to 20 hairlike cilia. The cilia waft in the layer of mucus coating the olfactory membrane and react to smells by generating a nerve impulse. The cilia from the lining of the nose (magnified above) form a dense carpet.

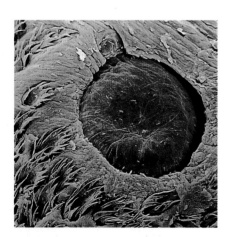

A question of taste

The vallate papillae form a V-shaped row at the back of the tongue. Each papilla (above in brown) measures about .07 in (1–2 mm) in diameter and contains up to 100 taste buds. Most taste buds are found in papillae, although some are also on the palate, throat, and epiglottis.

Organ of taste

The tongue's surface is rough because it is covered with small bumps called papillae. Taste buds are located in the walls of some of the papillae. Humans can detect four tastes – bitter, sour, salty, and sweet.

Epiglottis

Tonsil

Bitter

Sour

Salty

Sweet

Vallate papilla
Vallate papillae are the largest papillae. Taste buds are located along their sides.

Fungiform papilla
These mushroom-shaped papillae are scattered over the tongue. They have taste buds on the top.

Filiform papilla
Large numbers of these tiny papillae are arranged in rows over the tongue. They do not contain taste buds.

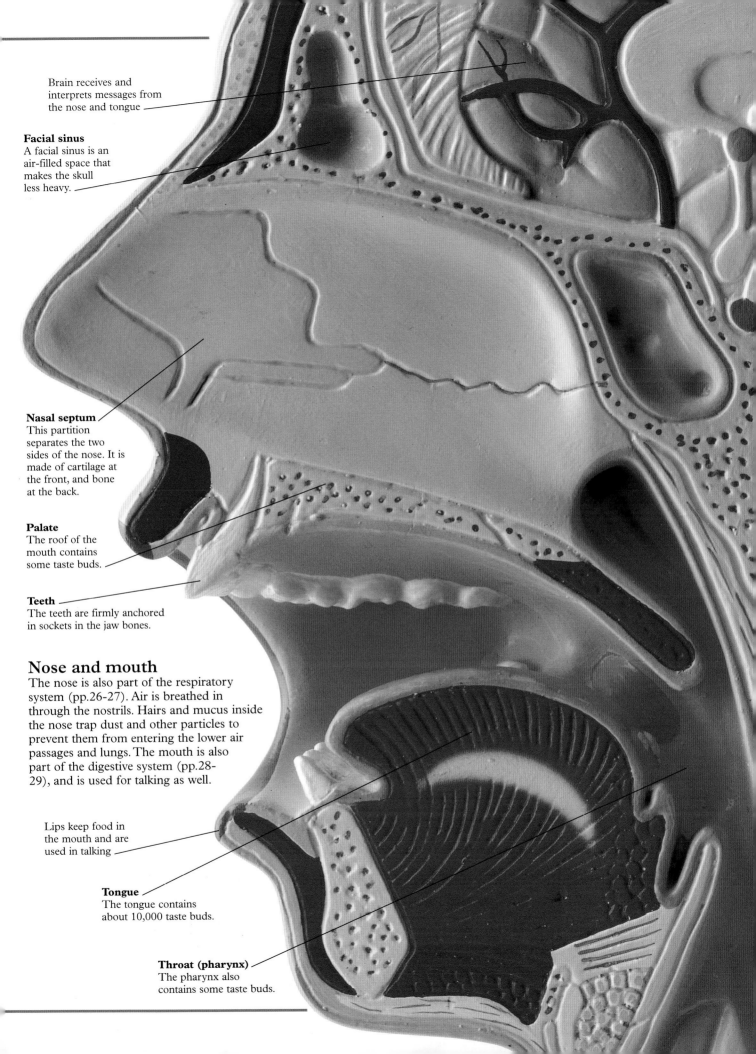

Brain receives and
interprets messages from
the nose and tongue

Facial sinus
A facial sinus is an
air-filled space that
makes the skull
less heavy.

Nasal septum
This partition
separates the two
sides of the nose. It is
made of cartilage at
the front, and bone
at the back.

Palate
The roof of the
mouth contains
some taste buds.

Teeth
The teeth are firmly anchored
in sockets in the jaw bones.

Nose and mouth
The nose is also part of the respiratory
system (pp.26-27). Air is breathed in
through the nostrils. Hairs and mucus inside
the nose trap dust and other particles to
prevent them from entering the lower air
passages and lungs. The mouth is also
part of the digestive system (pp.28-
29), and is used for talking as well.

Lips keep food in
the mouth and are
used in talking

Tongue
The tongue contains
about 10,000 taste buds.

Throat (pharynx)
The pharynx also
contains some taste buds.

Sight and sound

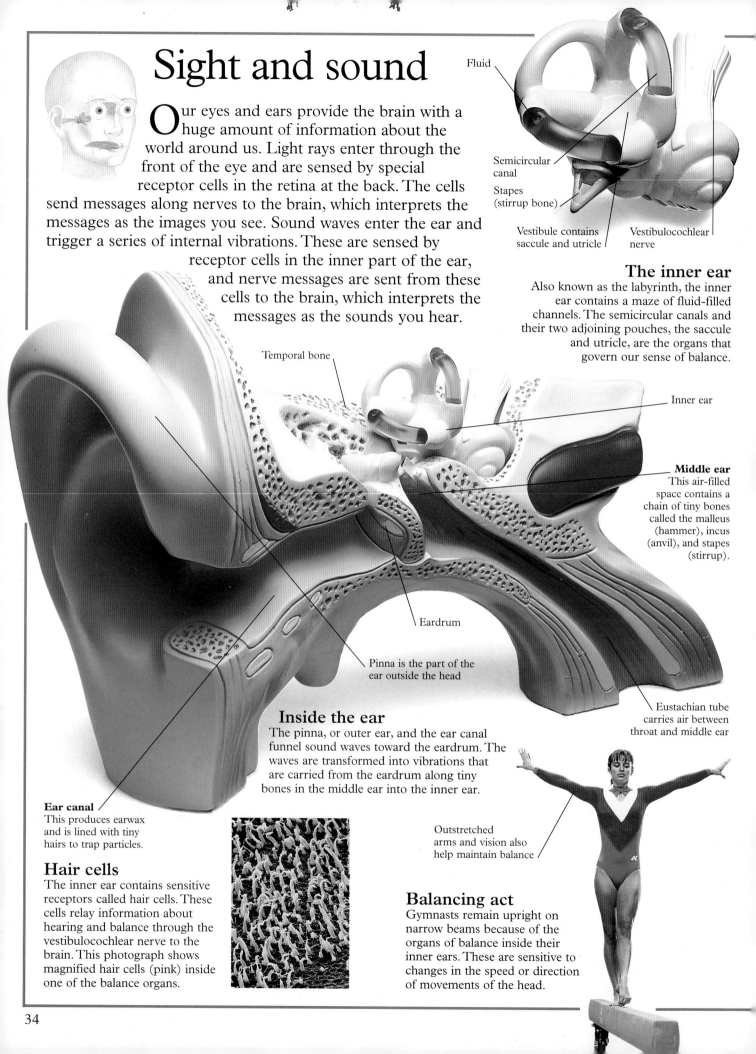

Our eyes and ears provide the brain with a huge amount of information about the world around us. Light rays enter through the front of the eye and are sensed by special receptor cells in the retina at the back. The cells send messages along nerves to the brain, which interprets the messages as the images you see. Sound waves enter the ear and trigger a series of internal vibrations. These are sensed by receptor cells in the inner part of the ear, and nerve messages are sent from these cells to the brain, which interprets the messages as the sounds you hear.

Fluid

Semicircular canal

Stapes (stirrup bone)

Vestibule contains saccule and utricle

Vestibulocochlear nerve

The inner ear
Also known as the labyrinth, the inner ear contains a maze of fluid-filled channels. The semicircular canals and their two adjoining pouches, the saccule and utricle, are the organs that govern our sense of balance.

Temporal bone

Inner ear

Middle ear
This air-filled space contains a chain of tiny bones called the malleus (hammer), incus (anvil), and stapes (stirrup).

Eardrum

Pinna is the part of the ear outside the head

Eustachian tube carries air between throat and middle ear

Inside the ear
The pinna, or outer ear, and the ear canal funnel sound waves toward the eardrum. The waves are transformed into vibrations that are carried from the eardrum along tiny bones in the middle ear into the inner ear.

Ear canal
This produces earwax and is lined with tiny hairs to trap particles.

Hair cells
The inner ear contains sensitive receptors called hair cells. These cells relay information about hearing and balance through the vestibulocochlear nerve to the brain. This photograph shows magnified hair cells (pink) inside one of the balance organs.

Outstretched arms and vision also help maintain balance

Balancing act
Gymnasts remain upright on narrow beams because of the organs of balance inside their inner ears. These are sensitive to changes in the speed or direction of movements of the head.

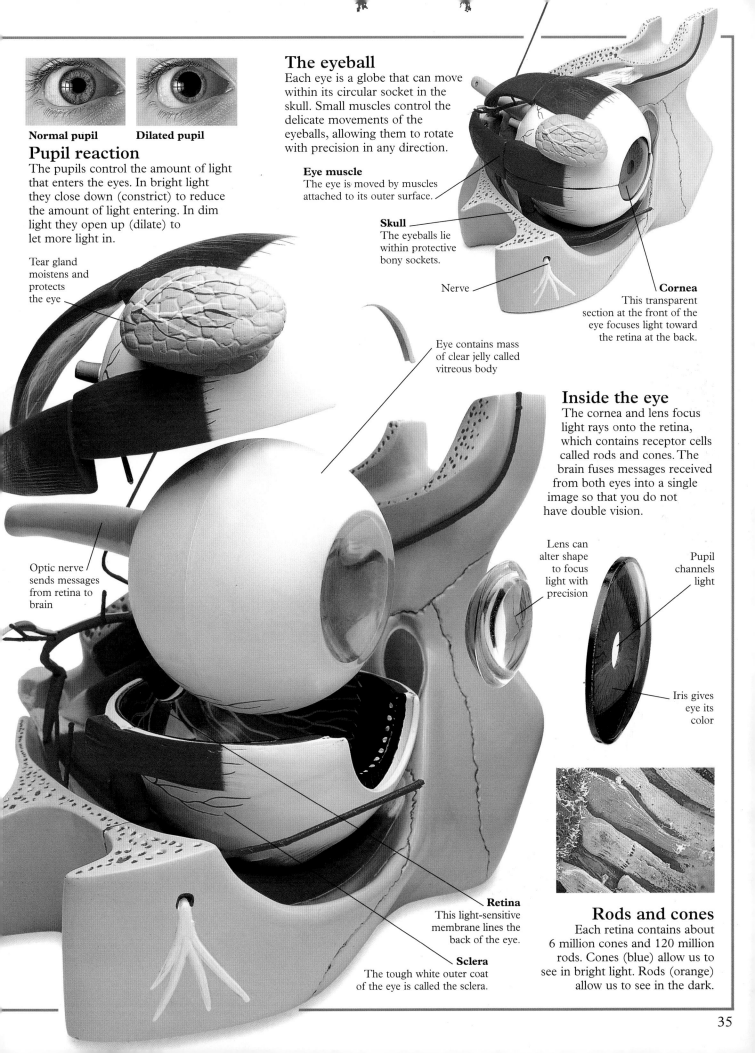

Normal pupil **Dilated pupil**

Pupil reaction

The pupils control the amount of light that enters the eyes. In bright light they close down (constrict) to reduce the amount of light entering. In dim light they open up (dilate) to let more light in.

Tear gland moistens and protects the eye

Optic nerve sends messages from retina to brain

The eyeball

Each eye is a globe that can move within its circular socket in the skull. Small muscles control the delicate movements of the eyeballs, allowing them to rotate with precision in any direction.

Eye muscle
The eye is moved by muscles attached to its outer surface.

Skull
The eyeballs lie within protective bony sockets.

Nerve

Cornea
This transparent section at the front of the eye focuses light toward the retina at the back.

Eye contains mass of clear jelly called vitreous body

Inside the eye

The cornea and lens focus light rays onto the retina, which contains receptor cells called rods and cones. The brain fuses messages received from both eyes into a single image so that you do not have double vision.

Lens can alter shape to focus light with precision

Pupil channels light

Iris gives eye its color

Retina
This light-sensitive membrane lines the back of the eye.

Sclera
The tough white outer coat of the eye is called the sclera.

Rods and cones

Each retina contains about 6 million cones and 120 million rods. Cones (blue) allow us to see in bright light. Rods (orange) allow us to see in the dark.

Skin, hair, and nails

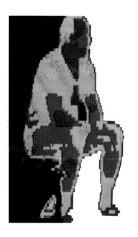

Skin is one of the body's organs. It covers the body's entire surface, protecting it from injury and infection. It is waterproof and contains a dark pigment called melanin, which protects against damage from strong sunlight. People with dark skin have a lot of melanin, people with light skin have less. Skin helps control body temperature, for example by sweating, and special nerve endings in the skin called sensory receptors are designed to detect touch, heat, cold, and pain. Skin also contains keratin, a tough protein present in hair and nails.

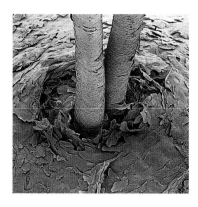

A close look
These hairs are emerging from follicles – pits surrounding the hair roots – in the scalp. Dead skin cells are constantly peeling from the surface of the skin like flakes of old paint.

Changing body temperature
These images are thermograms (heat photographs) of a squash player before a game (left) and after (right). The cool purples and blues are in sharp contrast to the hot reds, yellows, and whites (very hot).

Arrector pili muscle
Tiny arrector pili muscles pull hairs upright and produce goose pimples when you are cold or frightened.

Blood vessels
Veins and arteries help regulate body temperature by narrowing to conserve heat and widening to lose heat.

Subcutaneous layer
This layer beneath the skin contains fatty tissue that helps insulate the body.

Sebaceous gland
These glands are connected to hair follicles and make an oil called sebum, which coats the skin's surface.

Hair root

Root of nail   Nerve   Artery

Lunule
(crescent at
base of nail)

Nail fold

Bone

Hard as nails
Nails are hard plates that grow from the skin at the ends of your fingers and toes. The growing root of the nail is overlapped by skin called the nail fold. Your fingernails shield the sensitive skin underneath.

Cuticle
(rim of nail fold)

Nail

Vein

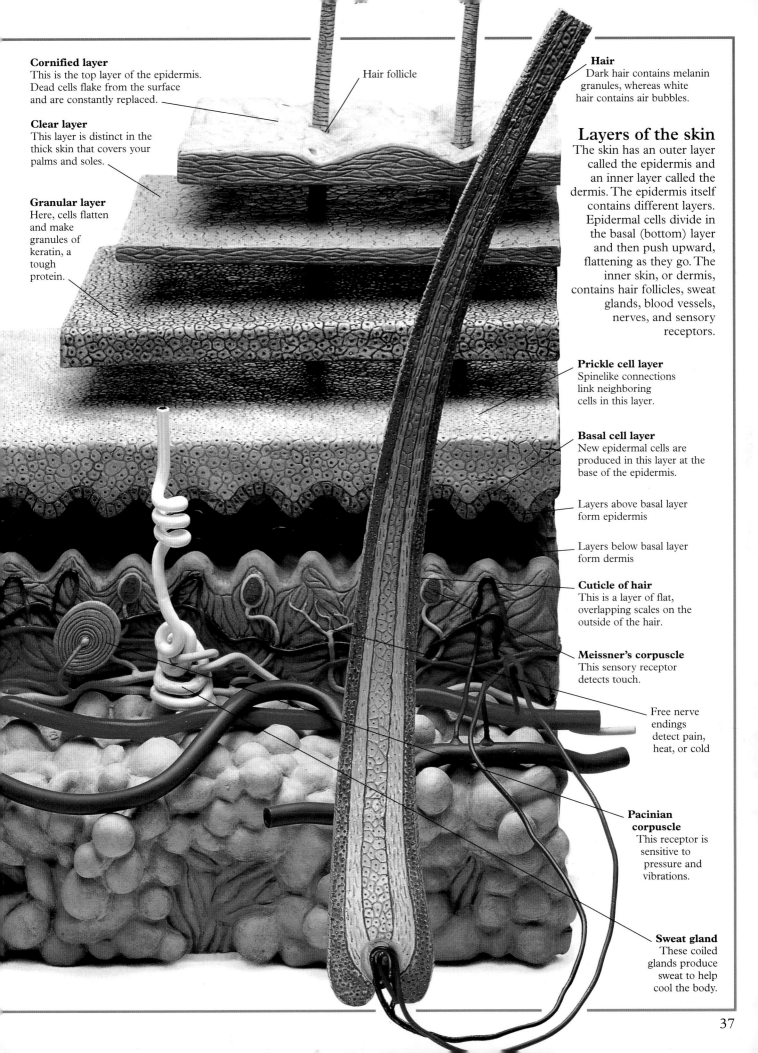

Cornified layer
This is the top layer of the epidermis. Dead cells flake from the surface and are constantly replaced.

Clear layer
This layer is distinct in the thick skin that covers your palms and soles.

Granular layer
Here, cells flatten and make granules of keratin, a tough protein.

Hair follicle

Hair
Dark hair contains melanin granules, whereas white hair contains air bubbles.

Layers of the skin
The skin has an outer layer called the epidermis and an inner layer called the dermis. The epidermis itself contains different layers. Epidermal cells divide in the basal (bottom) layer and then push upward, flattening as they go. The inner skin, or dermis, contains hair follicles, sweat glands, blood vessels, nerves, and sensory receptors.

Prickle cell layer
Spinelike connections link neighboring cells in this layer.

Basal cell layer
New epidermal cells are produced in this layer at the base of the epidermis.

Layers above basal layer form epidermis

Layers below basal layer form dermis

Cuticle of hair
This is a layer of flat, overlapping scales on the outside of the hair.

Meissner's corpuscle
This sensory receptor detects touch.

Free nerve endings detect pain, heat, or cold

Pacinian corpuscle
This receptor is sensitive to pressure and vibrations.

Sweat gland
These coiled glands produce sweat to help cool the body.

The reproductive system

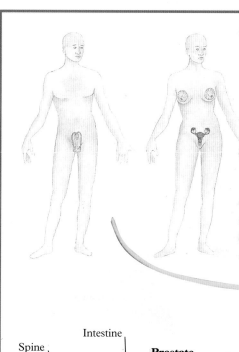

The reproductive system is made up of sexual organs, which do not become fully developed until the teenage years, when both boys' and girls' bodies change and grow rapidly. In males, the reproductive system includes the penis and a pair of glands called testes. In females, the system includes the uterus, vagina, and a pair of glands called ovaries. The testes produce male reproductive cells called sperm; the ovaries produce female reproductive cells called ova, or eggs. Each new life begins when a man's penis transfers sperm to the woman's body during sexual intercourse.

Journey of the sperm

Sperm are made in tiny tubes within the testes and are stored in a coiled tube called the epididymis. During sexual intercourse, sperm are pushed along another tube called the vas deferens.

Vas deferens
These two tubes carry sperm from each epididymis to the prostate.

Prostate

Epididymis

Testis

Urethra
This is a passage for sperm, and for urine from the bladder.

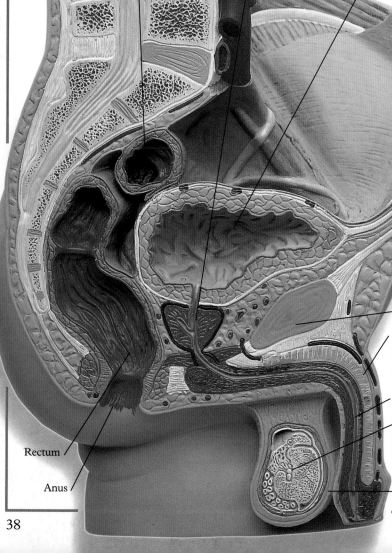

Spine

Intestine

Prostate
The prostate and seminal vesicles produce fluids that mix with sperm.

Bladder
The bladder is a muscular bag for the storage of urine.

Pubic bone

Rectum

Anus

Penis

Urethra

Testis

Scrotum

Male sex organs

The two testes hang behind the penis in a pouch of skin called the scrotum. The penis contains columns of spongy tissue that can fill with blood. When this happens, the penis becomes hard and erect, and can be inserted into a woman's vagina for intercourse.

Tail of a sperm
The sperm has a whip-like tail that enables it to swim, rather like a tadpole. After sexual intercourse, sperm swim from the vagina, through the uterus, to the fallopian tubes.

Penis
The penis transfers sperm into a woman's vagina during sexual intercourse.

Testis
The testes are egg-shaped glands that produce sperm and a male sex hormone called testosterone.

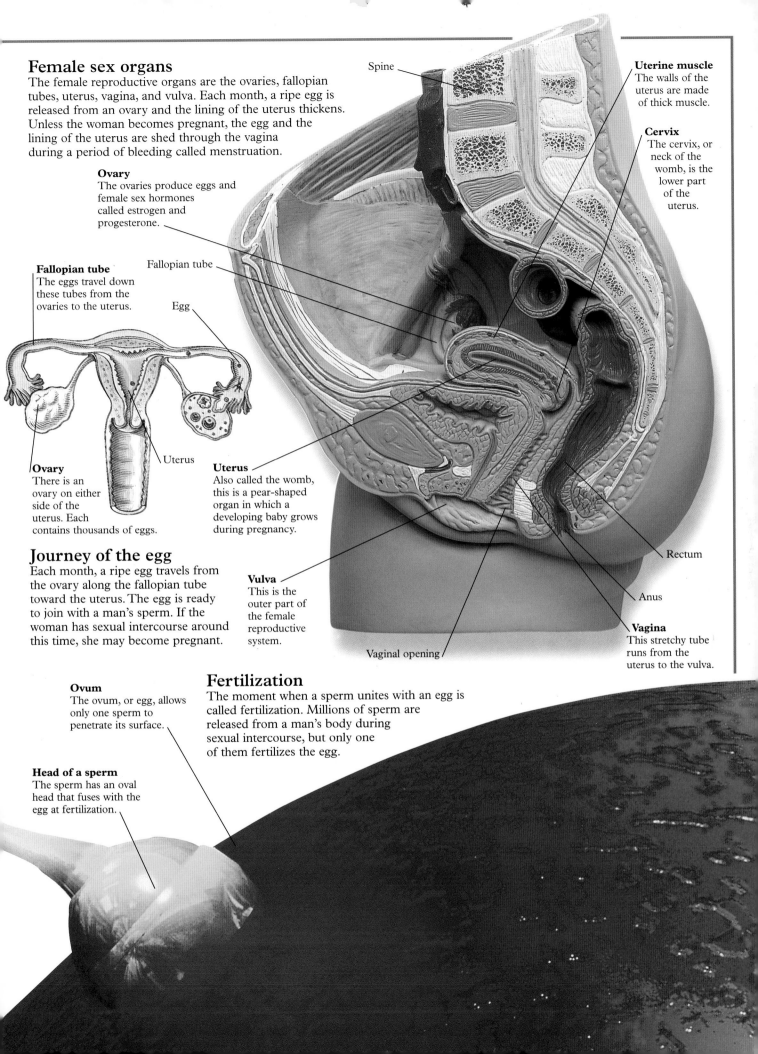

Female sex organs

The female reproductive organs are the ovaries, fallopian tubes, uterus, vagina, and vulva. Each month, a ripe egg is released from an ovary and the lining of the uterus thickens. Unless the woman becomes pregnant, the egg and the lining of the uterus are shed through the vagina during a period of bleeding called menstruation.

Ovary
The ovaries produce eggs and female sex hormones called estrogen and progesterone.

Fallopian tube
The eggs travel down these tubes from the ovaries to the uterus.

Egg

Fallopian tube

Uterus

Ovary
There is an ovary on either side of the uterus. Each contains thousands of eggs.

Uterus
Also called the womb, this is a pear-shaped organ in which a developing baby grows during pregnancy.

Journey of the egg

Each month, a ripe egg travels from the ovary along the fallopian tube toward the uterus. The egg is ready to join with a man's sperm. If the woman has sexual intercourse around this time, she may become pregnant.

Vulva
This is the outer part of the female reproductive system.

Spine

Uterine muscle
The walls of the uterus are made of thick muscle.

Cervix
The cervix, or neck of the womb, is the lower part of the uterus.

Rectum

Anus

Vagina
This stretchy tube runs from the uterus to the vulva.

Vaginal opening

Fertilization

The moment when a sperm unites with an egg is called fertilization. Millions of sperm are released from a man's body during sexual intercourse, but only one of them fertilizes the egg.

Ovum
The ovum, or egg, allows only one sperm to penetrate its surface.

Head of a sperm
The sperm has an oval head that fuses with the egg at fertilization.

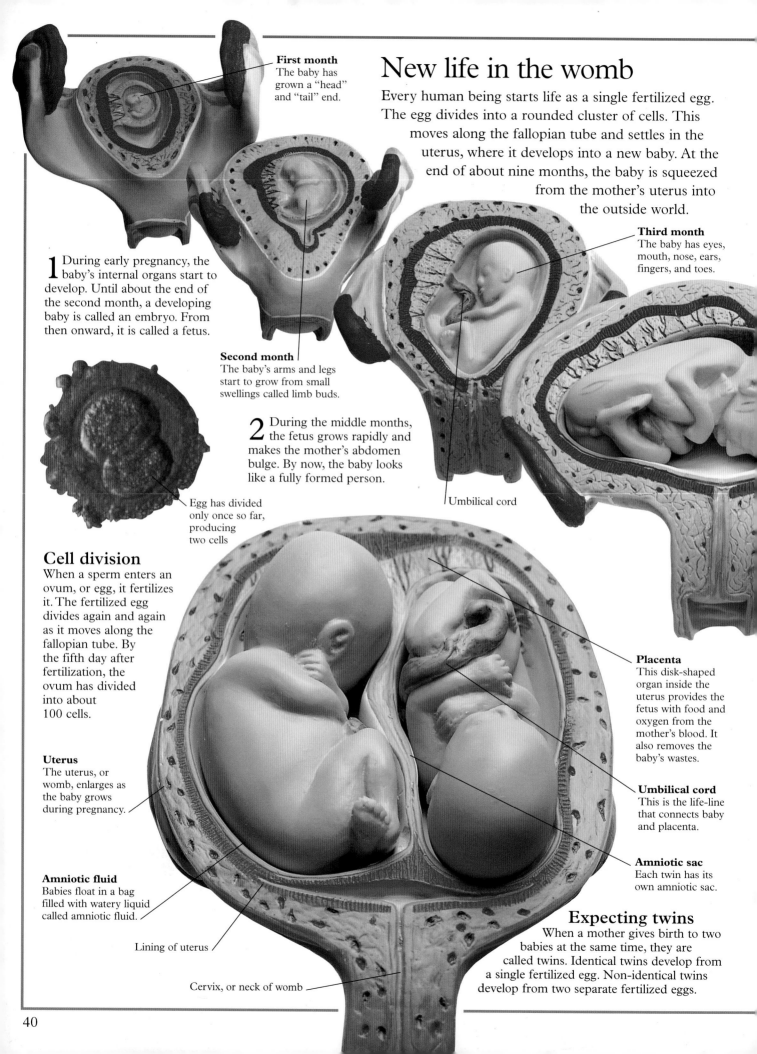

New life in the womb

Every human being starts life as a single fertilized egg. The egg divides into a rounded cluster of cells. This moves along the fallopian tube and settles in the uterus, where it develops into a new baby. At the end of about nine months, the baby is squeezed from the mother's uterus into the outside world.

First month
The baby has grown a "head" and "tail" end.

1 During early pregnancy, the baby's internal organs start to develop. Until about the end of the second month, a developing baby is called an embryo. From then onward, it is called a fetus.

Second month
The baby's arms and legs start to grow from small swellings called limb buds.

2 During the middle months, the fetus grows rapidly and makes the mother's abdomen bulge. By now, the baby looks like a fully formed person.

Third month
The baby has eyes, mouth, nose, ears, fingers, and toes.

Umbilical cord

Egg has divided only once so far, producing two cells

Cell division

When a sperm enters an ovum, or egg, it fertilizes it. The fertilized egg divides again and again as it moves along the fallopian tube. By the fifth day after fertilization, the ovum has divided into about 100 cells.

Uterus
The uterus, or womb, enlarges as the baby grows during pregnancy.

Placenta
This disk-shaped organ inside the uterus provides the fetus with food and oxygen from the mother's blood. It also removes the baby's wastes.

Umbilical cord
This is the life-line that connects baby and placenta.

Amniotic fluid
Babies float in a bag filled with watery liquid called amniotic fluid.

Amniotic sac
Each twin has its own amniotic sac.

Lining of uterus

Expecting twins
When a mother gives birth to two babies at the same time, they are called twins. Identical twins develop from a single fertilized egg. Non-identical twins develop from two separate fertilized eggs.

Cervix, or neck of womb

Breast before pregnancy

Fatty tissue

Milk duct

Nipple

Breast during pregnancy

Increased fatty tissue

Milk duct

Enlarged milk gland

Milk production

During pregnancy, the woman's breasts enlarge as they prepare to produce milk to feed the new baby. After the birth, the glands first produce a liquid food, colostrum, that is rich in minerals and protein. Then the breast milk comes through, providing all the nourishment a newborn baby needs.

Seventh month
The baby is almost fully mature. He or she grows bigger during the remaining months of pregnancy.

Muscles of uterus contract during childbirth to push baby out

Fourth month
The baby often turns somersaults inside the uterus during early and middle pregnancy.

3 In later pregnancy, the fetus reaches full maturity in preparation for life outside the mother's body. During childbirth, the cervix opens and the baby is pushed out through the vagina. The placenta is pushed out soon afterward.

Fifth month
The baby's skin is covered with a layer of fine, soft hair. The eyelids remain closed.

Mucus plug
A plug of mucus blocks the cervix during pregnancy.

Head down
During late pregnancy, the baby usually settles into an upside-down position, ready to be born headfirst.

Identical twins
Because they develop from the same fertilized egg, identical twins inherit the same characteristics. They are the same gender and look very similiar.

Amniotic sac
The fetus is surrounded by a fluid-filled bag of membranes called the amniotic sac.

Glossary

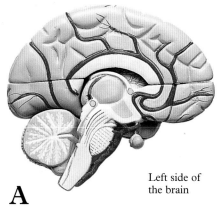

Left side of the brain

A

Adrenaline A hormone produced by the adrenal gland; it speeds the heartbeat and prepares the body for action.

Alveolus One of the tiny air sacs that exchanges oxygen and carbon dioxide in the lungs.

Artery A blood vessel that carries blood away from the heart.

B

Bacteria A large group of single-celled microscopic organisms.

Biceps brachii The muscle at the front of the upper arm.

Brain stem The lowest part of the brain; it controls automatic functions like breathing.

Bronchial tree The tunnel of branching tubes through which air moves into and out of the lungs.

CD

Calcium A mineral that gives hardness to teeth and bones.

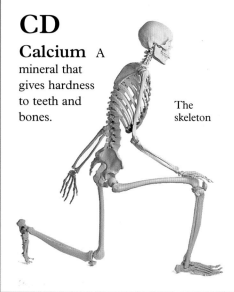

The skeleton

Carbon dioxide The waste gas produced when oxygen is used to burn food for energy. Carbon dioxide is breathed out by the lungs.

Cartilage A tough tissue, also known as gristle, cartilage is attached to the ends of bones.

Cerebellum The part of the brain, behind the brain stem, that helps control balance and movement.

Cerebrum The largest part of the brain, divided into two halves called the cerebral hemispheres.

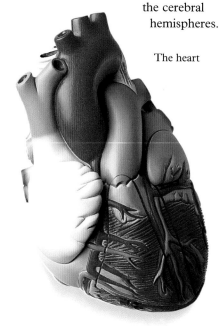

The heart

Cervix The neck of a body part, usually the uterus (womb).

Circulation The flow of blood around the body, pumped by the heart through arteries and veins.

Diaphragm The large, dome-shaped muscle that separates the chest from the abdomen.

EFG

Embryo An unborn infant in its early stages of development.

Epidermis The outer layer of the skin; it covers the inner layer, or dermis.

Esophagus The tube that leads from the mouth to the stomach.

Feces The waste products of digestion formed in the large intestine.

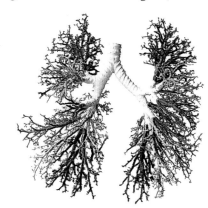

Bronchial tree

Fetus An unborn infant from about the third month of pregnancy until birth.

Gland An organ that makes and releases substances needed by the body. For example, an endocrine gland releases hormone into the blood.

HL

Hormone A chemical messenger that is released into the blood by a gland and has a particular effect on other parts of the body.

Hypothalamus A part of the brain that controls many functions of the nervous system and hormones.

Lens The transparent part of the eye just behind the iris, which is the colored part of the eye.

Ligament A tough band of tissue that holds bones together in a joint.

M

Medulla The inner part of an organ, such as the kidneys or adrenal gland; also part of the brain stem.

Membrane A thin layer of tissue that lines or covers part of the body.

Menstruation Monthly "period" of bleeding that occurs in women when the lining of the uterus (womb) is shed.

Motor neuron A nerve cell that relays messages from the brain and spinal cord.

Mucus A slimy fluid produced by mucous glands in membranes, for example in the nose.

Muscle contraction The shortening of muscle fibers that makes part of the body move or change shape.

NOP

Nerve A bundle of fibers that carries messages to and from the brain or spinal cord.

Neuron A nerve cell that can receive and transmit a signal.

Oxygen The gas that passes from air into blood in the lungs for use by body tissues to burn food for energy.

Pinna The part of the ear on the outside of the head.

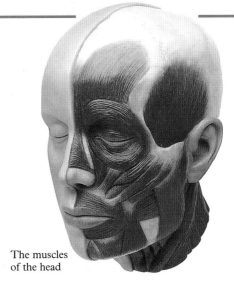

The muscles of the head

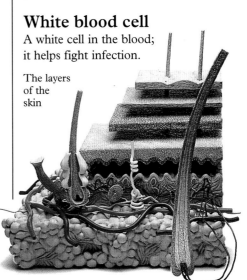

Cross-section of the ear

Protein One of many complex substances that help build the body.

Pulse The expansion of an artery as blood pumps through it.

R

Receptor cell A cell that receives information about body sensation and

responds by producing a nerve signal.

Red blood cell A red disk-shaped cell in the blood; it carries oxygen to body tissues.

Reflex An automatic reaction to a particular change in the body that is detected by a sense receptor.

Respiration The process by which oxygen reaches body tissues to produce energy and by which waste carbon dioxide is removed. The gases are exchanged by breathing.

S

Saliva The watery fluid released in the mouth, saliva aids chewing, tasting, and the body's digestion.

Scalp The skin covering the top of the skull, the scalp is where the hair of the head grows.

Semicircular canals Three channels in the inner ear that, with their adjoining pouches, govern our sense of balance.

Sensory neuron A nerve cell that relays messages to the spinal cord about the body's sensations.

Sperm Produced in the testes of a male, sperm combines with an egg inside a female to produce a baby.

Sweat glands Coiled glands in the skin that produce sweat to help cool the body.

T

Taste bud A group of taste receptor cells found on the tongue, the palate, the throat, and epiglottis.

Tendon A strong bundle of fibrous tissue that joins a muscle to a bone.

Testes The male sexual organs that produce sperm for reproduction.

Tissue A collection of similar cells that have the same function, for example muscle tissue.

Trachea The tube connecting the throat to the bronchi entering the lungs; also called the windpipe.

UVW

Urethra The tube that carries urine from the bladder out of the body.

Urine The waste fluid of the body that is produced by the kidneys.

Vein A blood vessel that returns blood to the heart.

Ventricle One of the two lower chambers of the heart. The left ventricle pumps fresh blood to the body through the aorta; the right ventricle pumps used blood to the lungs through the pulmonary artery.

White blood cell
A white cell in the blood; it helps fight infection.

The layers of the skin

Index

Acknowledgments

The publisher would like to thank the following for making or providing additional models:
Paul Binhold, Lehrmittelfabrik GMBH 38; 39; 40-41
Jeremy Hunt 16-17
Chris Reynolds, Maria Hurley, and Justin Bevan of BBC Visual Effects 15; 36; 36-37

Design assistance:
Emma Bowden, Darren Troughton
Photographic assistance:
Caroline Williams
Illustrations:
Patrizia Donaera 19b; 20; 25; introductory illustrations on spreads Simone End 21
Bill Le Fever 13; 19t; 27
John Woodcock 22; 24; 26; 32t; 32b; 38; 39; 41

Picture Credits
Key: l=left, r=right, t=top, c=center, a=above, b=below
The Image Bank: /Dan Heringa 41bl; /John P. Kelly 12br; /William Sallaz 34 br
Oxford Scientific Films: /D. Bromhall 40cl
Science Photo Library: 13tc; Prof J. Bories; /BSIP-VEM 32cl; /Prof S. Cinti, Universite D'Ancone 31br; /CNRI 15tl; 29br; /Ken Eward 20cr; /Simon Fraser 22cl; /Adam Hart-Davis 35tl; 35tlc; 36cla; 36ca; /Phil Jude 15br; /Mehau Kulyk 38c-39bc; /Scott Lamazine 13ca;

/Bill Longcore 35br; /Prof. P. Motta 17tl; 29tl; 32bl; 34bl; /NIBSC 24cra; /David Scharf endpapers; 36tr; /L. Steinmark 22bc; /Andrew Syred 25tr
Tony Stone Images: /RNHRD NHS Trust 13bc
Every effort has been made to trace the copyright holders. Dorling Kindersley apologises for any unintentional omissions and would be pleased, in such cases, to add an acknowledgement in future editions.
Index: Marion Dent

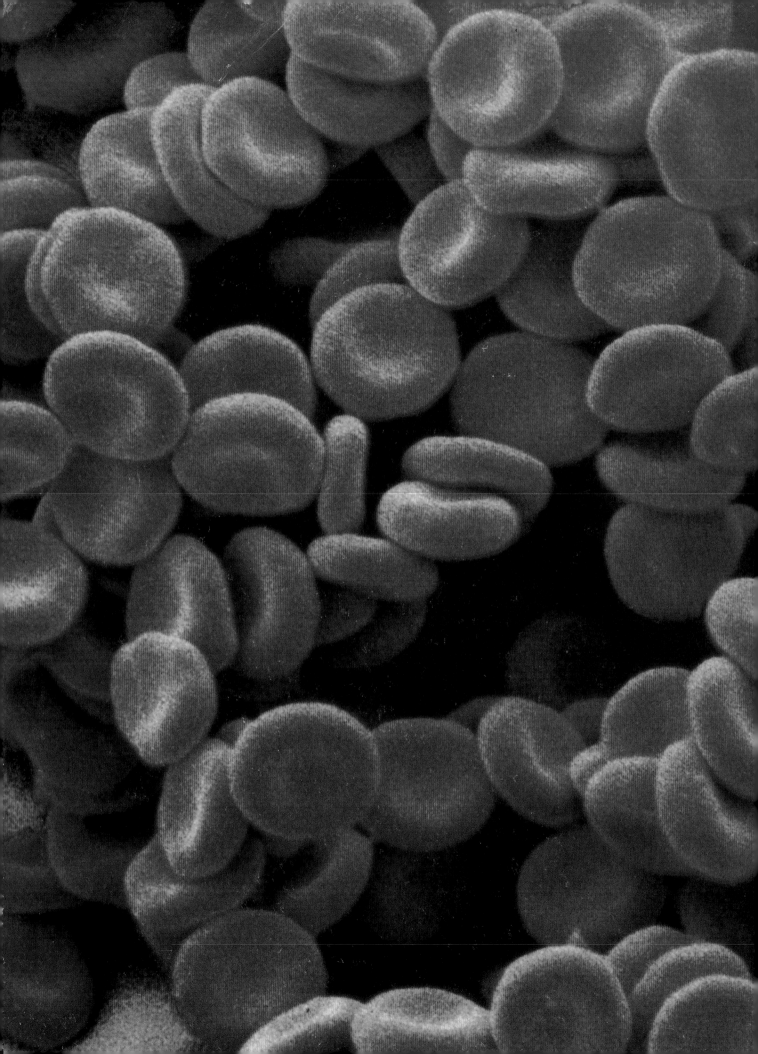